Sweet Vietnamese Bakes

A Dessert Lover's Tour of Southeast Asia

Tara Nguyen

Creator of TARA's Recipes

PAGE STREET
PUBLISHING CO.

PAGE STREET
PUBLISHING CO.

Copyright © 2023 Tara Nguyen

First published in 2023 by
Page Street Publishing Co.
27 Congress Street, Suite 1511
Salem, MA 01970
www.pagestreetpublishing.com

Distributed by Macmillan, sales in Canada by The Canadian Manda Group.

27 26 25 24 23   1 2 3 4 5

ISBN-13: 978-1-64567-809-0
ISBN-10: 1-64567-809-1

Library of Congress Control Number: 2022950282

Cover and book design by Elena Van Horn for Page Street Publishing Co.
Photography by Tara Nguyen

Printed and bound in the United States of America

Dedicated to all the Vietnamese food lovers,

tropical-flavor enthusiasts and dessert aficionados around the world. May this book inspire those who love baking and cooking at home, as well as those who want to learn about the cultural diversity and cuisine of their own and other countries. And a special thank-you to those who have loved and supported TARA's Recipes throughout the years; this book is my heartfelt expression of gratitude for your unwavering encouragement.

Contents

Breads and Bao Buns 107

Boba, Jellies and Ice Creams 133

Introduction

To my beloved readers,

Thank you for choosing to pick up this book and explore the delicious world of Vietnamese sweets and desserts with me. As a proud child of Vietnam, I have had the privilege of growing up surrounded by a variety of natural products and a rich cuisine that has been passed down through generations. It is my honor to be able to share this part of my culture with you through this book.

As someone who is passionate about food and specializes in researching the unique culinary features of my country, I am confident that the recipes in this book will take you on an exciting journey of discovery. You will not only learn about the historical and cultural significance of traditional cakes and desserts, but also about the fusion of culinary influences from other cultures, such as French, Chinese and Southeast Asian.

I have spent months crafting and writing these recipes, which I hope will not only provide a feast for your eyes but also inspire you to explore new ways of cooking and incorporating tropical ingredients into your dishes. Whether you are a seasoned chef or a beginner in the kitchen, I hope that you will find something in this book that piques your interest and satisfies your sweet tooth.

But this book is not just about food—it is about sharing a part of my culture with you and fostering a deeper understanding and appreciation for Vietnamese cuisine. I invite you to take a journey with me through the pages of this book, and to experience the richness and diversity of Vietnamese sweets and desserts.

Lastly, I would be thrilled to hear your thoughts and see your creations. Please feel free to share them with me on my social media platforms. On Facebook and YouTube you can find me under the pages TARA's Recipes. On Instagram you can tag me under the handle @taras.recipes and on TikTok @taras_recipes. I hope that you will find this book to be a source of inspiration and a gateway to a new culinary adventure.

Thank you for your support, and happy cooking!

With warm regards,

Tara Nguyen

Traditional Cakes

Vietnamese traditional cakes are a true reflection of the country's culture and way of life. The tropical climate and wet rice-farming culture are the main influences on the ingredients used in these cakes, which include rice, glutinous rice, bananas, coconuts, beans, cassava and pandan leaves, among other things. The natural ingredients used in Vietnamese traditional cakes give them a humble yet unforgettable flavor that is deeply ingrained in the hearts and minds of those born and raised in this small, S-shaped country. They are preserved and handed down from generation to generation, serving as a beautiful symbol of the country's ethnicity and cultural traditions.

Most of the cakes in this chapter are associated with my childhood, and they evoke a sense of comfort and remembrance. I grew up with them, enjoying them all with love. I still remember the excitement I felt every time my mom bought me a small piece of cake. I would hold it in my hand, inhale the fragrant scent, my eyes bright, and then slowly indulge myself. The sweetness would spread in my mouth, and I would savor the rich aroma of familiar and close ingredients. These cakes were a source of happiness for me and other children growing up in the countryside. The joy of those simple and idyllic times is forever etched in my memories, and every time I eat these cakes, I am transported back to those carefree days.

Banana Bread Pudding Cake (Banh Chuoi Nuong)

Vietnamese banana bread pudding cake is a beloved traditional dessert. The cake has a rich banana aroma and a delightful blend of flavors. For the best results, Nam Wah bananas (also called Chuoi Siam in Vietnam) are recommended for their sweet, juicy and fragrant flesh, but regular bananas will work as well. The cake is traditionally made with *banh mi*, the Vietnamese Baguette (page 109), which can be found in Asian grocery stores. If unavailable, white or French bread can be used as a substitute.

Yield:
6 servings

2 lb (905 g) ripe bananas

½ cup (100 g) sugar

½ tsp salt

¼ cup (60 ml) rum or red wine

4 oz (115 g) day-old bread, sliced

2 large eggs

½ cup (50 g) rice flour

½ cup (120 ml) sweetened condensed milk

½ cup (120 ml) milk

¾ cup (180 ml) coconut milk

½ cup (120 ml) + 1 tbsp (15 ml) melted unsalted butter, divided

Neutral oil, for pan

To reduce any bitter flavor, peel and soak the bananas in lightly salted water for 5 minutes. Then, place them in a large bowl with the sugar, salt and rum, and lightly mix to let the sugar melt and absorb quickly. Cover the bowl with plastic wrap and refrigerate for 6 hours or overnight to marinate. The longer the bananas marinate, the better their baked color will be.

In a nonstick skillet, cook the marinated bananas over medium-low heat for 15 minutes, stirring gently to avoid burning or smashing. Remove two-thirds of the bananas. Divide the cooked bananas you removed in half. For one half, slice each banana lengthwise. For the other half, cut them into disks. Mash the remaining cooked bananas with the liquid in the pan.

Next, preheat the oven to 210°F (100°C) and toast the sliced bread for 20 minutes to make it crispy, which will help it absorb liquid better.

In a large bowl, beat the eggs, then add the rice flour and stir well. Add the condensed milk, milk, coconut milk, ½ cup (120 ml) of the melted butter and the mashed bananas, and mix until smooth. Tear the bread into 1-inch (2.5-cm) pieces and soak it in the mixture for 15 to 20 minutes.

In the meantime, oil an 8-inch (20-cm) round cake pan and preheat the oven to 320°F (160°C). Spread half of the cake batter evenly in the pan, then add the lengthwise-cut bananas. Repeat with the rest of the batter, spreading it out evenly and then topping it with the banana disks. Brush the remaining 1 tablespoon (15 ml) of melted butter on top.

Bake the cake on the second rack from the bottom of the oven for 90 to 100 minutes. If you notice that the top of the cake is evenly golden during baking, cover it with foil and continue to bake for the remaining time. Once done, remove from the oven and let cool to room temperature while still in the pan.

The cake will have its best flavor after being chilled in the fridge for a day. Store any leftover cake in an airtight container at room temperature for up to a day, or in the fridge for up to 4 days. To reheat, bake at 340°F (170°C) for about 7 minutes, or microwave for 15 seconds.

Honeycomb Cakes (Banh Bo Nuong)

Honeycomb cake is a Vietnamese delicacy that is known for its soft and pliable texture, slight sweetness and creamy coconut milk flavor. The cake is named after the many small holes inside that resemble honeycombs, which the Vietnamese call "bamboo roots." The cake's signature aroma comes from the use of palm sugar, a specialty ingredient in southwest Vietnam. Baking with palm sugar fills the kitchen with a scent that's hard to resist. The traditional way to make this cake involves soaking the rice, making rice wine (a fermented rice drink popular in Vietnam) and letting the batter ferment. My recipe here is a faster way to make the cake that still maintains its full flavor. If you have the chance to visit Vietnam, I recommend trying the original version to fully experience its unique deliciousness.

Yield:
4 servings

Honeycomb Cake

8 oz (225 g) palm sugar

2 tbsp (30 ml) water

½ tsp salt

1 cup (240 ml) canned coconut milk

1¾ cups (210 g) tapioca starch

4½ tbsp (30 g) rice flour

2 large eggs, beaten

2 tsp (10 ml) vanilla extract

2 tbsp (30 ml) melted coconut oil

Neutral oil, for pan

2 tsp (9 g) baking powder

1 tsp baking soda

To make the cake, in a small saucepan, heat the palm sugar, water and salt over medium heat, swirling the pan regularly until the sugar dissolves. Avoid using a spoon to stir, to prevent sugar crystallization. Once the mixture is simmering, add the coconut milk, stir until incorporated, then turn off the heat and let the mixture cool to about 100°F (35°C).

For the batter, in a medium-sized bowl, stir together the tapioca starch and rice flour, pour in the warm sugar mixture and stir well. Add the beaten eggs and vanilla, stirring gently to combine. Sift the mixture twice through a fine-mesh sieve to remove lumps, returning the batter to its bowl. Then, add the melted coconut oil and stir gently to combine. Cover the bowl with plastic wrap and let rest for at least 20 minutes.

In the meantime, preheat the oven to 400°F (200°C). Select two 6-inch (15-cm), 2-inch (5-cm)-deep oval cake pans or a 7-inch (18-cm) round cake pan. Brush the bottom of the pans with neutral oil, but not the sides. Heat the prepared pans in the preheated oven for 10 minutes.

Just before baking, add the baking powder and baking soda to the batter. Remove the heated pans from the oven and quickly pour the batter through a sieve into the pans to create "bamboo roots" for the cake.

Lower the oven temperature to 360°F (180°C). Bake the cake on the second rack from the bottom of the oven for 10 minutes right away (do not wait for the oven to lower temperature first), then lower the heat to 320°F (160°C) and continue to bake for 40 more minutes. Once done, turn off the oven, flip the cakes upside down directly on the oven rack and let them rest in the oven for 30 minutes with the door slightly open to prevent the cakes from deflating due to heat shock.

(continued)

Honeycomb Cakes (Continued)

Coconut Milk Sauce

1 cup (240 ml) canned coconut milk

½ cup (120 ml) milk

½ cup (120 ml) sweetened condensed milk

Pinch of salt

4 tsp (10 g) cornstarch

5 pandan leaves (optional)

Toasted sesame seeds, for serving

To make the coconut milk sauce, in a small saucepan, combine the coconut milk, milk, condensed milk, salt and cornstarch, then heat over medium-low heat and stir until well mixed. Add the pandan leaves at this point, if desired, and stir the mixture for 5 to 7 minutes, or until it thickens. Then, remove from the heat and set aside to cool completely before serving.

Cut the honeycomb cake into 1-inch (2.5 cm)-thick slices and transfer them to a serving dish. Drizzle the coconut milk sauce over the cake slices and sprinkle toasted sesame seeds on top as a garnish.

The honeycomb cake is best enjoyed warm, so it's recommended to serve it right away. Store any leftover cake in an airtight container at room temperature for up to a day, or in the fridge for up to 4 days. To reheat, bake at 340°F (170°C) for about 7 minutes, or microwave for 15 seconds.

Pandan and Mung Bean Layer Cake or "Pig Skin Cake" (Banh Da Lon)

Yield: 6 servings

"Pig skin cake" is a well-known and beloved dessert from southern Vietnam that consists of layers of green and yellow cakes made from four major ingredients: pandan leaves, mung beans, coconut milk and tapioca starch. The cake has a unique texture that is both supple and creamy, and it's a feast for the eyes with its beautiful green and yellow layers. Vietnamese kids love peeling off the layers and savoring the contrasting textures of the green and yellow cakes. This is a sweet treat that you shouldn't miss when visiting Vietnam.

Yellow Layer

4 oz (115 g) peeled split mung beans, soaked in water for 4 hours, then drained

2 cups (475 ml) water

Pinch of salt

⅓ cup + ½ cup (200 ml) coconut milk

½ cup (60 g) tapioca starch

½ cup (100 g) sugar

1 tsp vanilla extract

¼ tsp neutral oil

Green Layer

1.5 oz (40 g) pandan leaves, chopped

⅔ cup (160 ml) water

⅔ cup (80 g) tapioca starch

½ cup (50 g) rice flour

½ cup (100 g) sugar

½ tsp salt

⅓ cup + 1 tbsp (95 ml) coconut milk

½ tsp neutral oil

½ tsp pandan extract, or 3 drops green + 1 drop yellow food coloring (optional)

Neutral oil, for pan

To make the yellow layer, in a small saucepan, combine the drained mung beans, water and salt, and bring to a boil over medium heat, skimming off any white foam that forms on the surface. Then, lower the heat to medium-low, cover and let simmer for 20 minutes, or until the beans become tender. Then, remove from the heat and set aside to cool.

In a blender, combine the cooked mung beans, coconut milk, tapioca starch, sugar and vanilla, and blend until smooth. Strain the mixture through a fine-mesh sieve into a small bowl to remove any lumps. Stir in the oil and cover the batter with plastic wrap while preparing the green layer.

To make the green layer, in a blender or small food processor, blend the chopped pandan leaves with the water until fine. Next, put the mixture in a nut milk bag or piece of cheesecloth and squeeze it over a small bowl to get the pandan juice. Measure out ⅔ cup (160 ml) of the pandan juice to use in the recipe.

(continued)

In a medium-sized bowl, stir together the tapioca starch, rice flour, sugar and salt. Add the pandan juice, coconut milk and oil to the center and stir until everything is well mixed. You may add pandan extract or food coloring to enhance the cake's color, if preferred. Lastly, use a fine-mesh sieve to strain the mixture into a second bowl to obtain a smooth batter.

Prepare a steamer with boiling water. Cover the lid with a thin, clean towel to prevent water from leaking into the cake while steaming. Oil a 7-inch (18-cm) round cake pan and steam it for 5 minutes.

Before you add the batter, stir it well so that the starch doesn't sink to the bottom of the bowl. Spread ⅓ cup (80 ml) of the green cake batter evenly in the cake pan, cover with the prepared lid and steam for 5 minutes. Then, add 1 cup (240 ml) of the yellow batter, spread it evenly, cover and steam for 5 minutes. Repeat with the remaining cake layers, alternating them and making sure to top the cake with the green batter. Continue to steam the cake for 30 minutes after the last layer is added. Check the doneness by inserting a toothpick into the center of the cake; if it comes out clean, the cake is done. Remove from the steamer and let cool.

After cooling the cake, refrigerate it for at least 6 hours before serving. To unmold the cake, run a thin knife along the edges of the pan, then invert the cake onto a dish. Cut the cake into bite-sized pieces and serve. Store any leftover cake in an airtight container at room temperature for up to a day, or in the fridge for up to 4 days. When you are ready to serve, you can take the cake from the fridge and eat it right away if you want it cold, or let it sit out at room temperature for about 5 minutes first.

Baked Cassava Cake (Banh Khoai Mi Nuong)

Cassava is a common tropical ingredient in Vietnamese sweets and desserts, and this baked cassava cake is one of them. Its main ingredients are cassava and coconut milk, which give it a mildly sweet and rich flavor, a fragrant and enticing smell and a soft and flexible texture. It's a great option for afternoon tea or a quick snack before the main course.

2 oz (60 g) peeled split mung beans, rinsed, then soaked in water for 4 hours, rinsed again, then drained

1 cup (240 ml) water

Pinch of salt

2 lb (905 g) cassavas, peeled, soaked for 6 hours, then drained

Neutral oil, for pan

1 cup (120 g) tapioca starch

½ cup (100 g) sugar, or to taste

1 large egg, beaten

½ cup (120 ml) sweetened condensed milk

2 tbsp (30 ml) melted unsalted butter

1 tsp vanilla extract

2 cups (475 ml) canned coconut milk

In a small saucepan, combine the drained mung beans, fresh water and salt, and bring to a boil over medium heat, skimming off any white foam that forms on the surface. Then, lower the heat to medium-low, cover and let simmer for 20 minutes, or until the beans become tender. Then, remove from the heat and, in a blender, blend the beans until smooth.

Next, grate the drained cassavas to ensure a fine texture and remove the woody core. Alternatively, you can cut the cassavas into small pieces, cover them with water and blend them to a smooth consistency for a faster process, but this method may affect the final texture of the cake.

Once the cassavas have been grated or blended, put the mixture in a piece of cheesecloth and squeeze it over a bowl to extract the liquid. Discard the cassava pulp. Set the liquid aside for 1 hour to allow the starch to settle. Afterward, carefully pour off and discard the water above the settled starch. Adding this starch to the cake will improve its texture and flavor.

Preheat the oven to 360°F (180°C). Oil the bottom and sides of an 8 x 6-inch (20 x 15-cm) rectangular cake pan and line the bottom with a piece of parchment paper.

In a medium-sized bowl, stir together the grated cassavas, cassava starch, mung bean puree, tapioca starch and sugar. Then, add the beaten egg, condensed milk, butter and vanilla, and mix until well combined. Finally, add the coconut milk and mix until incorporated.

Pour the cake batter into the prepared pan and smooth the top. Bake on the second rack from the bottom of the oven for 70 to 90 minutes. If you notice that the cake's surface is evenly golden during baking, cover it with foil and continue to bake for the remaining time.

The cassava cake is best enjoyed warm, so it's recommended to serve it right away. Store any leftover cake in an airtight container at room temperature for up to a day, or in the fridge for up to 4 days. To reheat, bake at 340°F (170°C) for about 7 minutes, or microwave for 15 seconds.

Steamed Rice Cakes (Banh Bo Hap)

Banh bo is a beloved spongy and soft cake composed of two primary ingredients: rice flour and coconut milk. It can be served with a creamy coconut milk sauce and toasted sesame seeds on top, or with roasted pork at receptions in the southwest of Vietnam. The traditional recipe calls for fermented rice wine to help the cakes rise, but it's challenging to prepare in other countries; this recipe offers a quicker version that's just as tasty.

Yield:
16 cakes

2¾ cups (290 g) rice flour

⅓ cup (40 g) tapioca starch

¾ cup (150 g) sugar, divided

Pinch of salt

2 tsp (6 g) instant yeast

1 cup (240 ml) lukewarm water (about 105°F [40°C])

1 cup (240 ml) canned coconut milk

2 tsp (10 ml) melted coconut oil

Neutral oil, for molds

Coconut Milk Sauce (page 14), for serving

Toasted sesame seeds, for garnish

In a large bowl, combine the rice flour, tapioca starch, ¼ cup (50 g) of the sugar, salt and, at a distance from the salt, the instant yeast. Mix well. Pour the lukewarm water into the center and stir with a wooden spoon or spatula until fully absorbed. Knead the dough for 10 minutes with clean hands until it is smooth and flowable, with portions overlapping one another to form a ribbon. If you find that the dough has not reached the desired consistency, you can adjust the amount of lukewarm water or rice flour accordingly. Cover the bowl with plastic wrap and allow the dough to ferment in a warm place for 30 to 45 minutes, or until the dough doubles in size.

Meanwhile, in a small saucepan, combine the coconut milk and the remaining ½ cup (100 g) of sugar. Heat over medium heat, stirring occasionally, until the sugar dissolves and the mixture comes to a boil. Remove the pan from the heat and let cool to room temperature.

After the first fermentation of the batter, add the cooled coconut milk mixture to the batter and mix well. You can pass the mixture through a fine-mesh sieve into a large bowl to remove any lumps, if desired. Then stir in the coconut oil. Cover the bowl with plastic wrap and let the batter ferment for the second time in a warm place for 60 to 90 minutes, or until it expands to 2 to 2½ times its original size with many air bubbles on the surface.

Prepare a steamer with boiling water. Oil 16 cupcake molds or small heatproof cups with neutral oil and steam them for 5 minutes. Gently stir the batter to incorporate the starch that has sunk to the bottom of the bowl. Divide the cake batter equally among the prepared molds and steam over high heat for 15 to 20 minutes, or until cooked.

Once the cakes have finished steaming, remove from the steamer and let them cool completely inside their molds for about 10 minutes before turning them out. To serve, drizzle with coconut milk sauce and sprinkle with toasted sesame seeds. Any leftover cake can be stored in an airtight container in the fridge for up to 4 days. When you're ready to eat, let it rest at room temperature for 5 minutes or microwave for 15 seconds.

Hollow Donuts (Banh Tieu)

Yield:
14 donuts

Hollow donuts are a classic snack that you can easily find sold as street food in Vietnam. They are super tender, coated with crispy sesame seeds and have a hollow inside. *Banh tieu* is usually enjoyed warm after frying. Sometimes, they are filled with durian, sticky rice or fluffy steamed rice cake. You can definitely fill it with chocolate or any of your favorite fillings.

1 cup (240 ml) lukewarm milk or water (about 105°F [40°C])

8 tbsp (100 g) sugar, divided

2 tsp (6 g) instant yeast

3 cups (375 g) all-purpose flour, sifted

1 tbsp (12 g) baking powder

½ tsp salt

2 tbsp (30 ml) neutral oil, plus more for fermentation bowl and for frying

½ cup (70 g) white sesame seeds, for coating

In a small bowl, combine the lukewarm milk, 1 tablespoon (13 g) of the sugar and the yeast. Stir well and set aside for 10 minutes.

In a large bowl, whisk together the sifted flour, remaining 7 tablespoons (87 g) of sugar, baking powder and salt. Make a well in the middle and pour in the yeast mixture. Mix everything together with a wooden spoon or spatula until no dry flour remains.

Transfer the dough to a clean work surface and knead by hand for 10 minutes, or until smooth. Then, add the oil and keep kneading for another 10 minutes, or until the oil is fully mixed in and the dough is smooth, shiny and elastic. If you have a stand mixer, you can use it to knead the dough more easily. Form the dough into a round, smooth ball. Oil a large bowl and put the dough inside. Wrap the bowl with plastic wrap and let the dough rise in a warm place for 45 to 60 minutes, or until it has doubled in size.

After fermentation, take the dough out and press it to deflate the air inside. Then, divide the dough into 14 equal-sized portions. Roll each portion into a smooth round ball. Cover the balls with a damp, clean towel or plastic wrap to prevent drying.

In the meantime, pour the oil to a depth of 3 inches (7.5 cm) into a large, deep saucepan and heat over medium heat until it reaches 355°F (180°C). Take each ball of dough and roll it in the white sesame seeds to coat. Use a rolling pin to flatten each dough ball into a 4½-inch (11.5-cm) disk. Fry one disk at a time, flipping it every 5 to 7 seconds, using two wooden chopsticks or a spatula. The disk will puff up like a balloon. Keep flipping and frying until it turns golden brown. Remove the donut from the oil and transfer it to a paper towel–lined tray to remove any excess oil. Repeat with the remaining dough.

Serve while they are warm to fully enjoy their flavor. These donuts are best served on the same day, but you can store any leftovers in a ziplock bag or airtight container for up to 2 days, or in the fridge for up to 4 days. To reheat, you can bake them in the oven, fry them or use a microwave.

Sesame Balls (Banh Ran Me)

Sesame balls get their name from their appearance, which resembles a table tennis ball with a shell completely covered in sesame seeds. The ball has a crispy and chewy crust made from glutinous rice flour, with a filling of tender and creamy mung beans. In Vietnam, they are known as sesame donuts in the North and orange cakes in the South, and they are often associated with childhood memories. Sesame balls are also a common street food in Vietnam.

Mung Bean Filling

4 oz (115 g) peeled split mung beans, soaked in water for 4 hours, then drained

2 cups + ¼ cup (540 ml) water, divided

Pinch of salt

⅓ cup (67 g) sugar

2 tbsp (30 ml) melted coconut oil

1 tbsp (8 g) glutinous rice flour

To make the filling, in a medium-sized saucepan, combine the drained mung beans with 2 cups (480 ml) of the water and the salt. Bring to a boil over high heat, and skim off any white foam that forms on the surface. Then, lower the heat to medium-low, cover and let it simmer for 20 minutes, or until the beans become tender. Then, remove from the heat and stir the sugar into the mixture until well incorporated and smooth.

Pass the mixture through a fine-mesh sieve into a medium-sized nonstick skillet and stir over low heat until it boils. Add the coconut oil in two batches, mixing thoroughly after each addition. Next, in a small bowl, combine the glutinous rice flour with the remaining ¼ cup (60 ml) water, then gently stir it into the filling mixture. Keep stirring constantly for 15 to 20 minutes, or until the filling gets thick and can be shaped like dough and maintain its shape.

Once done, remove from the heat, transfer the filling to a heatproof container, cover with plastic wrap and let cool to room temperature. Once cooled, divide the filling into twenty equal-sized portions, each weighing ½ ounce (15 g). Roll them into smooth balls and cover with plastic wrap or a clean kitchen towel to prevent drying.

(continued)

Sesame Balls (Continued)

Sesame Dough

4 oz (115 g) peeled and cooked potato (any white starchy variety will work)

¼ cup (50 g) sugar

⅓ cup (80 ml) boiling water

1½ cups (180 g) glutinous rice flour

¾ cup (80 g) rice flour

1 tsp baking powder

½ cup (120 ml) hot water (about 175°F [80°C])

2 tsp (10 ml) melted coconut oil

½ cup (70 g) sesame seeds, for coating

Cooking oil, for frying

To make the dough, in a medium-sized bowl, mash the cooked potato until smooth, then add the sugar and boiling water and mix well.

In a large bowl, combine the glutinous rice flour, rice flour and baking powder. Make a well in the center and add the potato mixture, hot water and coconut oil. Mix together with a wooden spoon or spatula until no dry flour remains. Knead the dough until smooth, then cover with plastic wrap and let rest for 20 to 30 minutes. Then, divide the dough into twenty equal-sized portions, each about 1 heaping tablespoon (20 g). Roll them into smooth balls and cover them with plastic wrap or a clean kitchen towel to prevent drying. Place the sesame seeds on a small plate.

Take one dough ball, make an indentation in the center, insert a ball of filling and gently pull the sides of the dough up and around the filling, making sure there's no air inside. Pinch the dough together at the top, smooth out any seams, then shape back into a ball. Spray the dough ball with water (I use a spray bottle), then roll in the sesame seeds. Press around the dough ball with dry palms so that the sesame seeds stick firmly to the surface. Repeat with the rest of the filling and dough.

In the meantime, pour the oil to a depth of 3 inches (7.5 cm) into a deep, large saucepan and heat over medium heat until it reaches 250°F (120°C). Working in batches, carefully drop the sesame balls into the hot oil. Don't fry too many balls at once, because when the balls expand, they will stick together. Remember to turn the balls frequently during frying so that they expand and color evenly. After 20 to 25 minutes of frying, the balls will become golden brown. Remove the balls from the oil and transfer them to a paper towel–lined tray to absorb any excess oil. Repeat with the remaining sesame balls.

The sesame balls should be served while they are warm to fully enjoy their flavor. Store any leftovers in a ziplock bag or airtight container at room temperature for up to 2 days, or in the fridge for up to 4 days. To reheat, you can bake them in the oven, fry them or use a microwave.

Marble Pandan Rice Cake (Banh Duc La Dua)

Yield:
6 servings

Pandan rice cake is a rustic and popular Vietnamese sweet known for its smooth and flexible texture, sweet flavor when combined with sugar syrup and creamy richness of Coconut Milk Sauce (page 14). Its green layers, interspersed with white to create a marbled pattern, make for a delightful treat that is as enjoyable to make as it is to eat.

White Paste

½ cup (60 g) tapioca starch

½ cup (50 g) rice flour

2 tsp (9 g) granulated sugar

⅓ tsp salt

½ cup (120 ml) water

½ cup + 2 tbsp (150 ml) canned coconut milk

1 tsp melted coconut oil

Green Paste

1 oz (30 g) chopped pandan leaves

1 cup + 2 tbsp (270 ml) water, divided

½ cup (60 g) tapioca starch

½ cup (50 g) rice flour

2 tsp (9 g) granulated sugar

⅓ tsp salt

1 tsp melted coconut oil

3 drops green food coloring + 1 drop yellow food coloring (optional)

Neutral oil, for cake pan

To make the white paste, in a medium-sized bowl, combine the tapioca starch, rice flour, granulated sugar and salt. Pour the water, coconut milk and coconut oil into the center and stir until incorporated. Pass the mixture through a fine-mesh sieve into a medium-sized nonstick saucepan. Stir constantly over medium heat for 3 minutes, or until a few lumps form on the bottom, then remove from the heat. Continue to stir the mixture constantly until you get a smooth, sticky paste.

To make the green paste, use a blender to grind the chopped pandan leaves with ½ cup (120 ml) of the water until it becomes fine. Next, put the mixture in a piece of cheesecloth or nut milk bag and squeeze it over a small bowl to get the pandan juice. In a medium-sized bowl, combine the tapioca starch, rice flour, granulated sugar and salt. Pour the remaining ½ cup plus 2 tablespoons (150 ml) of water, pandan juice and coconut oil into the center and stir until well combined. If desired, at this stage you can add the food coloring to enhance the color of the cake. Pass the mixture through a fine-mesh sieve into a medium-sized nonstick saucepan, then cook the green paste in the same way as the white paste.

Prepare a steamer with boiling water. Cover the lid with a thin, clean towel to prevent water from leaking into the cake while steaming. Oil a 7-inch (18-cm) round cake pan to prevent the cake from sticking.

Pour the green paste into the prepared pan and spread it out evenly. Add the white paste on top and make a marble pattern by briefly swirling a wooden spoon or spatula through both layers (keeping the colors distinct, not blended). Steam the cake over medium heat for 30 minutes, or until fully cooked. To check whether the cake is done, insert a toothpick into the center down to the bottom. If it comes out clean, the cake is ready. If it's sticky, steam for a few more minutes. Once done, remove from the steamer and allow the cake to cool completely at room temperature, then cover with plastic wrap and chill in the fridge for 6 hours before serving.

(continued)

Marble Pandan Rice Cake (Continued)

Ginger Syrup

6 oz (170 g) palm sugar

½ oz (15 g) fresh ginger, sliced

¾ cup (180 ml) + 1 tbsp (15 ml) water, divided

1 tsp cornstarch

Coconut Milk Sauce (page 14), for serving

Toasted sesame seeds, for serving

To prepare the ginger syrup, in a small saucepan, combine the palm sugar, sliced ginger and ¾ cup (180 ml) of the water. Cook over medium heat for about 10 minutes, or until the sugar has dissolved. In a small bowl, mix the remaining 1 tablespoon (15 ml) of water with the cornstarch and slowly add it to the sugar syrup, stirring constantly until it thickens slightly. Cook for another 30 seconds before removing from the heat.

To serve, first cut the cake into bite-sized pieces and place them on a plate. Then, drizzle the ginger syrup and Coconut Milk Sauce over the cake and sprinkle with toasted sesame seeds. The cake can be stored in an airtight container in the fridge for up to 3 days. To enjoy the best flavor, reheat the leftover cake in a microwave for 20 seconds or steam for 5 minutes before eating.

Snowball Cakes: Vietnamese Coconut Peanut Mochi Balls (Banh Bao Chi)

Yield: 14 snowballs

These cakes originated in Chinese cuisine and were brought to Vietnam by immigrants. They have a soft and supple skin made from glutinous rice flour; are filled with a mixture of peanuts, roasted sesame and coconut; and are often covered with desiccated coconut or cooked glutinous rice flour. They are sold by street vendors but can also be found in upscale dim sum restaurants.

Coconut Filling

6 oz (170 g) shredded unsweetened coconut (preferably fresh)

⅓ cup (67 g) sugar

2 tbsp (30 ml) melted coconut oil

⅓ cup (50 g) toasted white sesame seeds

½ cup (70 g) crushed toasted peanuts

2 tsp (6 g) cooked glutinous rice flour

Skin

1 cup (120 g) glutinous rice flour

⅔ cup (67 g) rice flour

⅓ cup (67 g) sugar

⅓ tsp salt

1⅓ cups (320 ml) milk or water

2 tbsp (30 ml) neutral oil

2 tsp (6 g) cooked glutinous rice flour, for dusting

⅔ cup (60 g) desiccated coconut, for coating

To make the filling, in a medium-sized bowl, combine the shredded coconut and sugar and let sit for 30 minutes to infuse the sweetness. Then, transfer the mixture to a nonstick skillet, add the coconut oil and cook over medium-low heat, stirring constantly, until the steam evaporates and the coconut becomes dry and translucent. Mix in the toasted sesame seeds and peanuts, then add the cooked glutinous rice flour a little at a time and stir until the mixture is sticky and well mixed. Let the filling cool to room temperature before shaping it into fourteen equal-sized balls. Cover the filling balls with plastic wrap and refrigerate until needed.

To make the skin, in a separate medium-sized bowl, combine the glutinous rice flour, rice flour, sugar and salt. Pour in the milk and stir constantly until the mixture is thoroughly dissolved and well combined. Pass this batter through a fine-mesh sieve into another bowl to remove any lumps.

Cover the bowl of batter tightly with plastic wrap, then steam for 30 minutes over high heat. Alternatively, transferring the batter to a microwave-safe bowl, you can microwave it on high for 3 minutes, then mix it thoroughly and microwave again for another minute, or until the dough is fully cooked. Once finished, allow the dough to cool slightly before adding the oil, then mix well with a wooden spoon or spatula. Knead the dough with your hands until it becomes smooth and elastic.

Put the dough on a clean work surface and dust it with the cooked glutinous rice flour. Divide the dough into fourteen equal-sized portions, then form each into a ball.

To assemble, flatten out each dough ball with a rolling pin, put one filling ball in the middle and gently pull the sides of the dough up and around the filling. Pinch the dough together at the top and smooth out any seams. Coat the balls evenly with a layer of desiccated coconut.

Snowball cakes are best eaten the same day they are made, but they may be stored in an airtight container in the fridge and enjoyed up to 3 days later.

Steamed Banana Cake (Banh Chuoi Hap)

Steamed banana cake is a beloved dessert in the southern provinces of Vietnam, cherished for its chewy texture and the soft sweetness of ripe bananas. It's usually served with a rich, creamy Coconut Milk Sauce (page 14) and crispy roasted peanuts. Along with baked banana pudding cake, this cake is one of the two most popular types of rustic banana cakes in Vietnam.

2 lb (905 g) ripe bananas

⅓ cup (67 g) sugar

3 tbsp (20 g) rice flour

2 cups (240 g) tapioca starch

Pinch of salt

1 cup (240 ml) hot water (about 160°F [70°C])

2 drops yellow food coloring (optional)

Neutral oil, for pan

Coconut Milk Sauce (page 14), for serving

Crushed toasted peanuts, for garnish

Toasted sesame seeds, for garnish

To reduce any bitter flavor, peel and soak the bananas in lightly salted water for 5 minutes, then drain and allow them to dry. Cut the bananas into coins about 1⁄16 inch (2 to 3 mm) thick and put them in a bowl. Mix them slightly with the sugar and set aside for about 30 minutes to let the sugar absorb.

Into a medium-sized bowl, sift together the rice flour, tapioca starch and salt, and mix well. Slowly pour the hot water into the center of the flour while stirring continuously until the mixture is completely dissolved and combined. If desired, you can add yellow food coloring to enhance the color of the cake at this stage. Reserve about ½ cup (80 g) of the sugared banana slices for garnish and then carefully fold the remaining slices into the batter.

Prepare a steamer with boiling water. Cover the lid with a thin, clean towel to prevent water from leaking into the cake while steaming. Oil an 8-inch (20-cm) round cake pan to prevent the cake from sticking.

Pour the cake batter into the prepared pan and spread it evenly. Arrange the reserved banana slices on top. Steam the cake over medium heat for 35 to 45 minutes, or until fully cooked. To check whether the cake is done, insert a toothpick into the center, down to the bottom of the pan. If it comes out clean, the cake is ready. If it's sticky, steam for a few more minutes.

When the cake is done, remove from the steamer and let cool completely. To remove the cake from the pan, turn it upside down on a cutting board. Then, cut it into bite-sized pieces and place on a serving plate. Drizzle the cake with coconut milk sauce and sprinkle the peanuts and sesame seeds over the top.

This banana cake should be eaten throughout the day when it is still soft, chewy and fresh. If you must store it in the fridge, be sure to warm it in a microwave for about 20 seconds before eating.

Durian Mung Bean Cakes (Banh Pia Sau Rieng)

Yield:
8 cakes

Pia cake is a popular delicacy from the Soc Trang province in southwest Vietnam, introduced by Chinese immigrants. This cake is typically flat and round and has multiple layers of soft pastry encasing a filling of mung beans, durian and salted egg yolk. The cake boasts a rich and sweet flavor, and the distinct aroma of durian makes it highly addictive.

Filling

4 oz (115 g) peeled split mung beans, soaked in water for 4 hours, then drained

2 cups (480 ml) + 1 tbsp (15 ml) water, divided

Pinch of salt

⅓ cup (67 g) + 1 tbsp (13 g) sugar, divided

2 tbsp (30 ml) melted coconut oil

4 tsp (10 g) cornstarch

7 oz (200 g) durian flesh, mashed

8 salted egg yolks (see page 150)

¼ cup (60 ml) rice wine

1 tbsp (15 ml) sesame oil

To make the filling, in a medium-sized saucepan, cook the drained mung beans in 2 cups (480 ml) of the water and the salt. Bring it to a boil over high heat and skim off any white foam. Lower the heat to medium-low, cover and simmer the beans for 20 minutes, or until tender. Then, remove the pot from the heat and blend the mung beans, cooking water, and ⅓ cup (67 g) of the sugar until smooth.

Put the mixture through a fine-mesh sieve into a medium-sized nonstick skillet and stir over low heat until it boils. Add the coconut oil in two batches, mixing well after each addition. Next, in a small bowl, mix the remaining tablespoon (15 ml) of the water with the cornstarch and gently incorporate it into the filling. Stir for 15 to 20 minutes, or until the mixture thickens and can be formed into dough. Remove the pan from the heat, transfer the filling to a heatproof container, cover it with plastic wrap and let the filling cool to room temperature.

In a medium-sized nonstick skillet over low heat, stir the mashed durian flesh and the remaining tablespoon (13 g) of sugar until the sugar melts and the durian becomes translucent. Transfer the durian to a small bowl, cover with plastic wrap and set it aside.

Preheat the oven to 320°F (160°C). In a small bowl, soak the salted egg yolks in the rice wine for 5 minutes, then drain and rinse. Place the yolks on a tray and drizzle the sesame oil on top. Bake for 7 minutes.

Divide the mung bean filling into eight equal-sized portions and roll them into balls. Flatten each ball with your hands into a 3½-inch (9-cm) disk and top it with 1 tablespoon (15 g) of the durian filling. Place a salted egg yolk on each mung bean–durian seam. Place the assembled balls on a tray and wrap the tray with plastic wrap.

(continued)

Durian Mung Bean Cakes (Continued)

Mooncake Dough

2¾ cups (345 g) all-purpose flour, divided

¼ cup (50 g) sugar

⅓ tsp salt

½ cup (120 ml) melted lard, divided

⅓ cup (80 ml) water

¼ cup (30 g) tapioca starch

To make the mooncake dough, in a medium-sized bowl, make the outer (water) dough by mixing 2 cups (250 g) of the flour, sugar and the salt. Add ¼ cup (60 ml) of the lard and mix well. Pour in the water gradually and mix by hand until no dry flour remains. Transfer the dough to a clean work surface and knead for 7 to 10 minutes, or until smooth and elastic. Cover the dough with plastic wrap and let it sit for 15 to 20 minutes.

Next, in a separate small bowl, make the inner (oil) dough by mixing the remaining ¾ cup (95 g) of flour with the tapioca starch and the remaining ¼ cup (60 ml) of lard until the dough is uniform and smooth. Cover the dough with plastic wrap and let it rest for 15 to 20 minutes.

After it has rested, divide the outer dough into eight equal-sized pieces, each about 1 level tablespoon plus 1 heaping tablespoon (35 g total). Cover them with plastic wrap to keep them from drying out. Then, divide the inner dough into eight equal-sized pieces, each about 1 heaping tablespoon (19 g). Flatten the outer dough into a disk, put the inner dough in the middle and wrap the outer dough around it, pressing it closed at the seams. Cover them with plastic wrap and let them rest for 10 minutes.

Use a rolling pin to flatten one piece of dough, seam side down, into an oval or rectangular shape that is approximately ¼ inch (6 mm) thick. Flip the dough over and roll it up lengthwise. Next, turn it 90 degrees, flatten it and roll it up again. Repeat with the remaining dough pieces. Cover them with plastic wrap and let them rest for 10 minutes.

Preheat the oven to 340°F (170°C). Take one piece of dough, use your thumb and index finger to pinch two corners together in the middle, then do the same with the other two corners. Roll it out into a 4½- to 5-inch (12- to 13-cm) disk. Place the filling in the middle of the dough with the salted egg facing up, then re-form the dough to thoroughly surround the filling.

Red Mark and Egg Wash

10 drops red food coloring

2 tbsp + 1 tsp (35 ml) water, divided

1 large egg yolk

Place the cake seam-side down on a baking sheet lined with parchment paper. Use your palm to gently press down on the cake to make it a little bit flatter. Do the same thing with the rest of the dough and filling.

You can use a cookie press to give the cakes a traditional look, but it's optional. In a small bowl, mix the red food coloring with 2 tablespoons (30 ml) of the water and place a cotton pad or cotton ball inside to absorb the color. Dip the patterned side of the cookie press into the colored cotton pad and make a mark in the center of each cake. If you don't have a cookie press, use a little brush to dot red coloring in the center of each cake. Alternatively, feel free to draw any pattern you choose, such as flowers. Skip this step if you prefer plain cakes.

Bake the mooncakes on the middle rack for 20 minutes, then remove from the oven and let cool for 5 minutes. Whisk together the egg yolk and remaining teaspoon of water to create an egg wash. Brush the egg wash over the top of the cakes and bake for another 5 minutes.

To store the cakes, let them cool completely before placing them in an airtight container. They can be kept at room temperature for 2 to 3 days, or in the fridge for up to 1 week. If you want to store them longer, freeze them for up to a month and thaw them slowly before eating. They can be enjoyed cold or at room temperature, or heated in a microwave for 15 seconds.

Vietnamese Conjugal Cakes
(Banh Phu The / Banh Xu Xe)

Yield:
8 cakes

This is a traditional Vietnamese cake with a long history dating back to the Ly dynasty. According to legend, the cake was created by the queen for her husband, King Ly Anh Tong (r. 1138–1175), who was away at war, as a way to express her love. The cake was so delicious that the king named it *banh phu the* (conjugal cake) to commemorate their love. The cake's pandan leaf–infused transparent skin has a chewy texture and fragrant aroma, which pairs perfectly with the sweet and tender mung bean filling to create a distinctive and unforgettable Southeast Asian flavor.

Coconut Mung Bean Filling

4 oz (115 g) mung beans, soaked in water for 4 hours, then drained

2 cups (475 ml) water

Pinch of salt

¼ cup (50 g) sugar

⅓ cup (80 ml) canned coconut milk

1 tbsp (15 ml) melted coconut oil or neutral oil

Pandan Skin

2 oz (60 g) chopped pandan leaves

1¾ cups (420 ml) water

1⅔ cups (200 g) tapioca starch

¼ cup (50 g) sugar

½ tsp salt

2 oz (60 g) shredded unsweetened coconut (preferably fresh)

⅓ tsp pandan extract, or 3 drops green + 1 drop yellow food coloring (optional)

To make the filling, in a medium-sized saucepan, combine the drained mung beans with the water and salt. Bring to a boil over high heat, and skim off any white foam that forms on the surface. Then, lower the heat to medium-low, cover and let simmer for 20 minutes, or until the beans become tender. Then, remove from the heat, transfer the beans to a blender, add the sugar and coconut milk and blend together until smooth.

Pass the mixture through a fine-mesh sieve into a medium-sized nonstick skillet and stir over low heat until it boils. Add half of the coconut oil at a time, mixing thoroughly after each addition. Stir constantly for 15 to 20 minutes, or until the mixture gets thick and can be shaped like dough and maintain its shape. Then, remove the pan from the heat, transfer the filling into a heatproof container, cover with plastic wrap and let the filling cool to room temperature. Once cooled, divide the filling into eight equal-sized portions and roll them into balls. Cover them with plastic wrap and refrigerate until needed.

To make the skin, in a blender or small food processor, blend the chopped pandan leaves with the water until fine. Put the mixture in a piece of cheesecloth or a nut milk bag and squeeze over a small bowl to get the pandan juice. Measure out 1¾ cups (420 ml) of the pandan juice to use in the recipe.

In a medium-sized saucepan, mix together the tapioca starch, sugar, salt, pandan juice and shredded coconut. You may add pandan extract or food coloring to enhance the skin's color, if preferred. Place the saucepan over low heat and stir the mixture for 5 to 7 minutes, or until it gets thick and sticky like a paste. Remove from the heat and set aside to cool.

(continued)

Vietnamese Conjugal Cakes (Continued)

Neutral oil, for molds

Toasted sesame seeds, for garnish

To assemble the cake, use eight small heatproof bowls or silicone muffin cups as molds. Oil the molds with neutral oil and spread a tablespoon (15 g) of the skin paste in each. Divide the filling into eight equal-sized portions and place on top of the skin paste, then cover fully with another tablespoon (15 g) of skin paste.

Prepare a steamer with boiling water. Steam the cakes for 20 minutes over medium heat, or until the skin paste is translucent and you can see the filling. Once done, remove the cakes from the steamer and let cool slightly at room temperature.

Spread a layer of plastic wrap on a plate and sprinkle a few toasted sesame seeds in the middle. Remove a cake from its mold and place it in the middle of the plastic wrap. Wrap tightly with the plastic wrap to form a square cake with a smooth surface. Repeat with the remaining cakes.

After wrapping the cakes, allow them to cool completely, then serve, making sure to take the plastic wrap off first. They can be stored at room temperature for 2 to 3 days, or in the fridge for up to 5 days. When you are ready to eat, you can take the cake from the fridge and eat it right away if you want it cold, or you can let it sit out at room temperature for about 5 minutes.

5-Color Silkworm Cassava Cakes
(Banh Tam Khoai Mi Ngu Sac)

Yield:
6 servings

Cassava silkworm cake is a distinct and fascinating sweet that resembles silkworms with its colorful appearance. It is made by steaming cassava cake and then rolling it in desiccated coconut. The cake has a chewy texture, a mild sweetness and a delightful cassava fragrance. This cake is a common street food in Vietnam, particularly in the southern and southwestern regions.

Cassava Cake

2 lb (905 g) cassavas, peeled

¾ cup (90 g) tapioca starch

⅓ cup (67 g) sugar

⅓ tsp salt

½ cup (120 ml) canned coconut milk

1¼ cups (115 g) desiccated coconut

5 Colors (optional)

White: ¼ cup (60 ml) canned coconut milk

Blue: 10 dried butterfly pea flowers + ¼ cup (60 ml) boiling water

Green: ½ oz (15 g) chopped pandan leaves + ¼ cup (60 ml) water

Pink: ½ oz (15 g) beet + ¼ cup (60 ml) water

Yellow: ½ oz (15 g) carrot + ¼ cup (60 ml) water

To make the cake, soak the peeled cassavas in water for at least 6 hours or overnight. Next, grate them to ensure a fine texture and remove the woody core. (See a photo of this on the next page.) Alternatively, you can cut the cassavas into small pieces, cover them with water and use a blender to blend them to a smooth consistency for a faster process, but this method may affect the final texture of the cake.

Once the cassavas have been grated or blended, put the mixture in a piece of cheesecloth and squeeze it over a small bowl to extract the liquid. Reserve the cassava pulp. Set the liquid aside for 1 hour to allow the starch to settle. Afterward, discard the water above the settled starch. Adding this starch to the cake will improve its texture and flavor.

In a medium-sized bowl, combine the grated cassava, cassava starch, tapioca starch, sugar, salt and coconut milk, and mix well. Next, divide the mixture into five equal-sized portions and transfer each portion into a separate small bowl.

To dye the cake, start by stirring the coconut milk well and mixing it into one portion of the cassava batter to create the white dough. Next, create a blue batter by steeping butterfly pea flowers in ¼ cup (60 ml) of boiling water for 7 to 10 minutes, squeezing out the blue water and mixing it with a portion of the batter. To produce the other three colors, puree the pandan leaves, beet and carrot separately with their respective ¼ cup (60 ml) of water, strain their juice into separate small bowls through their own respective piece of cheesecloth and mix each juice with a different portion of the batter. In addition to using vegetables for natural colors, you can also use food coloring. Alternatively, if you prefer to keep the cake's original color, you can increase the amount of coconut milk by 1¼ cups (300 ml), added to the entire batter, and skip the dyeing step. (See a photo of this process on the next page.)

(continued)

5-Color Silkworm Cassava Cakes (Continued)

Toppings

2 tbsp (20 g) toasted white sesame seeds

2 tbsp (20 g) toasted peanuts, crushed

2 tbsp (26 g) sugar

⅓ tsp salt

To prepare the steamer, heat the water until it boils. If the steamer is large enough to steam all the dough at once, that's ideal. Otherwise, line five round heatproof plates or cake pans with parchment paper. Spread each batch of cake batter about ½ inch (1.3 cm) thick onto a plate/pan and steam each batch of cakes, one at a time, for 10 to 12 minutes, or until the cake turns translucent. After steaming, allow the cakes to cool slightly, then cut them into thin strips resembling silkworms. While the cakes are still warm, roll each color in ¼ cup (23 g) of desiccated coconut to ensure an even coating.

In a small bowl, mix together all of the topping ingredients. When ready to serve, sprinkle the topping mixture over the silkworm cakes and serve while they are still warm. Cassava silkworm cakes should be eaten throughout the day to keep them soft, chewy and fresh. If you must store them in the fridge, be sure to warm them in a microwave for 20 seconds before eating.

Mung Bean Mooncakes
(Banh Trung Thu Nuong Nhan Dau Xanh)

Yield:
10 cakes

During the mid-autumn season in Vietnam (around August of the lunar calendar), it is a tradition for people to make and give one another mooncakes as a symbol of family reunion and happiness. Mooncakes are typically round in shape, representing the full moon that illuminates the mid-autumn night. There are two main types of traditional baked mooncakes: sweet and savory. This recipe teaches you how to make a sweet mung bean mooncake, which is one of the most popular sweet fillings for baked mooncakes in Vietnam.

Mooncake Filling

8 oz (225 g) peeled split mung beans, soaked in water for 4 hours, then drained

1 qt (946 ml) + 2 tbsp (30 ml) water, divided

⅓ tsp salt

¾ cup (150 g) sugar

½ cup (120 ml) melted coconut oil or neutral oil

¼ cup (30 g) cornstarch

2 tbsp (30 ml) maltose

1 tsp vanilla extract (optional)

10 salted egg yolks (see page 150)

¼ cup (60 ml) rice wine

1 tbsp (15 ml) sesame oil

To make the filling, in a medium-sized saucepan, combine the drained mung beans with the quart (946 ml) of fresh water and salt, bring to a boil over high heat and skim off any white foam that forms on the surface. Then, lower the heat to medium-low, cover and let simmer for 20 minutes, or until the beans become tender. Then, remove from the heat and, in a blender, blend the cooked beans and sugar together until smooth.

Pass the mixture through a fine-mesh sieve into a large nonstick skillet. Stir constantly over medium heat until the mixture reaches a boil, then lower the heat to medium-low. Divide the coconut oil into three parts, and add them one at a time to the mixture, stirring until well combined before adding the next. Then, in a small bowl, combine the cornstarch with the remaining 2 tablespoons (30 ml) of water and gently stir it into the mixture. Lastly, add the maltose and stir until it's completely mixed.

Keep stirring the filling mixture for an additional 30 to 45 minutes, or until it starts to thicken slightly and no longer sticks to the pan. Then, lower the heat to low and add the vanilla extract (if using), then cook, stirring, for another 10 to 15 minutes, or until the mixture can be shaped like dough and maintain its shape. Remove from the heat, transfer the filling to a heatproof container, cover with plastic wrap and let cool to room temperature.

Meanwhile, heat the oven to 320°F (160°C). In a small bowl, soak the salted egg yolks in the rice wine for 5 minutes, then drain and rinse. Place the yolks on a tray and drizzle the sesame oil on top. Bake for 7 minutes. After the filling has cooled, divide it into ten equal-sized portions, each about ⅓ cup (85 g). Place a salted yolk in the middle of each portion of filling and shape it into a ball. Cover the filling balls with plastic wrap and refrigerate until needed.

(continued)

Mung Bean Mooncakes (Continued)

Mooncake Dough

½ cup (165 g) golden syrup (available on Amazon or in the baking aisle)

2 tbsp (30 ml) neutral oil, plus more for molds

1 tsp honey

1½ tsp (8 g) peanut butter

1 large egg yolk

2⅓ cups (292 g) all-purpose flour, sifted

¼ tsp baking soda

Egg Wash

1 large egg yolk

1 tsp water

½ tsp golden syrup or honey

½ tsp sesame oil

To make the mooncake dough, in a medium-sized bowl, mix together the golden syrup, oil, honey, peanut butter and egg yolk until well combined. Sift in the flour and baking soda, and mix until the flour has absorbed all the liquid. Knead quickly with your hands to form a smooth dough ball. Cover the dough with plastic wrap and let rest for 30 minutes at room temperature. Then, divide the dough into ten equal-sized balls, each consisting of about 3 heaping tablespoons (50 g). Cover them with a kitchen towel or plastic wrap to prevent them from drying out.

Preheat the oven to 375°F (190°C) and line a baking sheet with parchment paper. To assemble, take a ball of dough and roll it out with a rolling pin until it's about 4 inches (10 cm) in diameter. Put a ball of filling in the center of the dough, then gently pull the sides of the dough up and around the filling, making sure there's no air inside. Pinch the dough together at the top, smooth out any seams and shape the dough into a ball. Repeat with the rest of the filling and dough. Cover the assembled mooncakes with a clean kitchen towel or plastic wrap to prevent them from drying out.

Apply a light layer of neutral oil to the inside of your mooncake mold. Place a mooncake ball in the mold, then use your fingers to gently push and spread out the dough so that it is equally distributed inside the mold. Put the mold on a flat surface covered with parchment paper, press it down and hold it there for about 10 seconds. This will leave a clear pattern on the mooncake's surface. Repeat until all eight mooncakes are formed.

Place the mooncakes on the prepared baking sheet and bake for 10 minutes on the middle rack of the oven. Once done, remove the pan from the oven and immediately spray the mooncake's surface with a thin layer of water. Allow the mooncakes to cool completely for 15 to 20 minutes. Lower the oven temperature to 340°F (170°C).

In a small bowl, whisk the egg-wash ingredients together and strain to remove any lumps. When the mooncakes are fully cooled, brush a thin layer of egg wash over the top and edges, being careful not to obscure the pattern. Return them to the oven and bake for another 10 minutes. Repeat this process three times more, or until the cake is evenly golden brown.

Allow the mooncakes to cool fully at room temperature after baking. Store them at room temperature in an airtight container for 12 to 24 hours to soften them up before serving. Mooncakes can be kept at room temperature for about a week in a dry environment with low humidity, or refrigerated for up to a month.

Coconut Filling Snowskin Mooncakes
(Banh Trung Thu Deo Nhan Sua Dua)

During the mid-autumn festival season in Vietnam, snowskin mooncakes are also a popular traditional cake for family reunions, in addition to baked mooncakes. Compared to baked mooncakes, snowskin mooncakes are easier and quicker to make, and they are the only kind of mooncakes that have sweet fillings. The cake has a soft and chewy skin with a white color, and can be filled with a variety of sweet fillings, such as mung beans, red beans, taro, lotus seeds, coconut and so on. This recipe will showcase a beloved filling among Vietnamese people, which is the coconut filling.

Yield:
10 cakes

Coconut Filling

8 oz (225 g) shredded unsweetened coconut

⅓ cup (80 ml) sweetened condensed milk

½ cup (120 ml) canned coconut milk

¼ cup (35 g) toasted sesame seeds

¼ cup (30 g) cooked glutinous rice flour, plus more for dusting

Simple Syrup

¾ cup + 2 tbsp (210 ml) water

1 cup + 1 tbsp (213 g) sugar

⅛ tsp fresh lemon juice or cream of tartar

Snowskin

2 tsp (10 ml) neutral oil

2 tsp (10 ml) pomelo aroma extract or vanilla extract (you can find pomelo aroma extract on Amazon or in the baking aisle)

1½ cups (180 g) cooked glutinous rice flour, divided

To make the coconut filling, in a medium-sized bowl, combine the shredded coconut and condensed milk. Allow the mixture to sit for 30 minutes to infuse the sweetness, then transfer the mixture to a medium-sized nonstick saucepan and add the coconut milk. Cook over medium heat for 10 minutes until the mixture becomes hot and dry. Turn off the heat and mix in the toasted sesame seeds. Gradually add the cooked glutinous rice flour, stirring until well combined, then knead with your hands until you can form a nonsticky dough. Finally, divide into eight equal-sized balls, each consisting of about 2½ heaping tablespoons (50 g). (See the photo on the next page for an example.) Cover the balls with plastic wrap and refrigerate until needed.

To make the simple syrup, in a small saucepan, combine the water and sugar, and stir well to dissolve the sugar. Bring the mixture to a boil over medium-high heat and remove any foam that forms on the surface. Lower the heat to low and let simmer for 10 minutes. Then, add the lemon juice and gently swirl the pan to combine it with the syrup (do not stir). Continue to simmer the syrup for 5 minutes before turning off the heat. After the syrup has cooled completely, measure out 11 ounces (320 g) to use for the snowskin.

To make the snowskin, in a medium-sized bowl, combine 11 ounces (320 g) of the simple syrup, oil and pomelo aroma extract. Then, spoon and sprinkle the cooked glutinous rice flour into the bowl, stirring constantly with a whisk until the mixture becomes smooth before adding the next spoonful. As the mixture becomes thicker and stickier, switch to a spatula for easier handling. Continue to add spoon by spoon until you have added two-thirds of the cooked glutinous rice flour (120 g), then cover the bowl with plastic wrap and let rest for 5 minutes.

(continued)

Coconut Filling Snowskin Mooncakes (Continued)

Prepare a clean work surface and dust it with half of the remaining cooked glutinous rice flour (30 g). Then, transfer the dough paste to the floured surface and sprinkle the remaining cooked glutinous rice flour (30 g) on top of the dough. Next, use a dough cutter to fold the dough from the side to the center, allowing it to absorb the flour gradually. Keep folding until the dough becomes smooth and is no longer sticky. Then, roll the dough into a log and divide it into eight equal-sized portions, each weighing around 3 ounces (90 g). Cover the dough balls with plastic wrap or a kitchen towel to prevent them from drying.

To assemble the snowskin mooncakes, use one piece of dough at a time, dusting it with dry flour and flattening it with a rolling pin into a 4-inch (10-cm) disk. Next, place a ball of filling in the center of the dough, then gently pull the sides of the dough up and around the filling, making sure there's no air inside. Pinch the dough together at the top and shape the dough into a ball. Repeat this process with the rest of the dough and filling.

To mold the mooncakes, dust a thin layer of dry flour inside the mooncake mold. Place the mooncake dough in the mold and use your fingers to gently spread out the dough to evenly fill the mold. Let the dough sit for a few minutes to create a distinct pattern on the surface of the mooncake. Flip the mold over and tap the sides to carefully remove the mooncake.

Snowskin mooncakes should be kept in an airtight container at room temperature for 1 day before they are served. This will give the skin time to soften and become less sweet, clearer and more flexible. The snowskin mooncakes can be stored for up to 4 days at room temperature. It is not recommended to store them in the fridge, as the skin may become hard and lose its pliability.

Traditional Desserts

Along with the traditional cakes in the previous chapter, the sweet soups and desserts in this chapter will reveal the most rustic and simple culinary elements in Vietnam's culinary culture. Sweet soups can easily be prepared at home and customized based on available ingredients and taste preferences. Although the cooking methods and ingredients used in these sweet soups are basic, a little technique is required to bring out their best flavors. Cooking sweet soups is a wonderful family activity, bringing everyone together in the kitchen.

As one travels across the three regions of Vietnam, the taste of sweet soups also varies. In the North, where the climate is often chilly, sweet soups tend to have a gentle sweetness and are best enjoyed while still hot. In Central Vietnam, particularly in Hue, famous for its royal cuisine, sweet soups are made with the utmost care and precision, resulting in an exquisite and delicate taste. In the South, where the sun shines almost year-round and ingredients are abundant, sweet soups often have a sweet and rich flavor and are served with coconut milk and shaved ice.

In addition to the sweet soups featured in this chapter, Vietnam also has many other mouthwatering sweet soups that are worth exploring, such as:

- Lotus seed and longan sweet soup (che long nhan hat sen)
- Sweet corn pudding (che bap)
- Hyacinth bean sweet soup (che dau van)
- Mixed bean sweet soup (che dau thap cam)
- Sticky rice pudding with black-eyed peas (che dau trang)

If you ever get the chance to visit Vietnam, don't pass up the opportunity to try these incredible sweet soups!

Banana Sago Pudding (Che Chuoi Bot Bang)

Banana sago pudding is a popular and homey Vietnamese dessert that utilizes everyday ingredients found in most Vietnamese households. The dish is beloved for its simplicity and convenience yet delectable taste. The combination of sweet bananas, chewy sago and creamy coconut milk makes for a mouthwatering treat that is definitely worth trying.

1 lb (455 g) ripe bananas

¾ cup (150 g) sugar, divided

3 oz (85 g) sago (mini tapioca pearls)

2 oz (60 g) dried cassava sticks

2 cups (475 ml) water

2 cups (475 ml) canned coconut milk

¼ tsp salt

¼ cup (30 g) toasted peanuts, crushed

Peel the bananas and soak them in lightly salted water for an hour to make them less bitter. This step is optional, so if you're short on time, you may skip the soak. Drain the bananas and transfer them to a medium-sized bowl. Add ½ cup (100 g) of the sugar and mix gently. Set the mixture aside for 15 minutes to allow the sugar to absorb.

Soak the sago and dried cassava sticks in room-temperature water for about 2 hours, then drain.

In a medium-sized saucepan, bring the water to a boil over medium heat. Add the coconut milk and mix thoroughly. Then, add the sugared bananas, gently swirl and cook over medium heat. After cooking for about 5 minutes, add the sago, cassava sticks, remaining ¼ cup (50 g) of sugar and the salt. Cook for another 10 minutes, or until the sago and cassava sticks are soft. Remove the pan from the heat.

This banana sago pudding can be enjoyed warm or cold. Simply scoop it into a small bowl, sprinkle some crushed peanuts on top and enjoy!

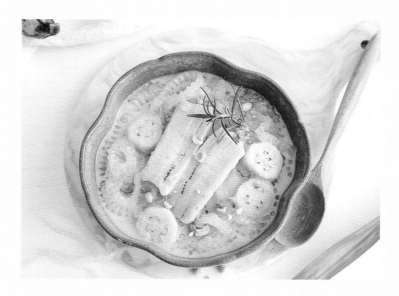

Mixed Fruit in Coconut Milk Dessert (Che Thai)

Yield: 6 servings

Che Thai is a dessert that originated in Thailand but has been adapted to suit the tastes of Vietnamese people over the years. A popular and refreshing sweet, particularly on hot days, it is made up of various fruits—such as jackfruit, longan and lychee—mixed with durian and served in coconut milk. The dish is known for its colorful appearance and rich, creamy taste.

Red Rubies

2 oz (60 g) beet, or 5 drops red food coloring mixed with 2 tbsp (30 ml) water

4 oz (115 g) water chestnuts, peeled and diced

2 tbsp (26 g) sugar, divided

½ cup (60 g) tapioca starch

Pandan Jelly

1 oz (30 g) chopped pandan leaves

2⅓ cups (560 ml) water, divided

1 tsp agar-agar powder

1 tsp konnyaku jelly powder (see page 150)

⅓ cup (67 g) sugar

Pinch of salt

Coconut Milk Soup

1⅔ cups (400 ml) canned coconut milk

¾ cup (180 ml) milk

½ cup (120 ml) sweetened condensed milk

Longan fruits, for serving

Jackfruit, for serving

Durian, for serving

Shaved ice, for serving

To make the red rubies, grate the beet, place in a piece of cheesecloth and squeeze out the juice into a medium-sized bowl. Alternatively, replace the beet juice with the red food-coloring mixture. Add the water chestnuts and 1 tablespoon (13 g) of the sugar and mix well. Let soak for 30 minutes, then drain the water chestnuts in a sieve to remove any excess liquid. Place them back in the bowl and combine them with the tapioca starch to fully coat. Sift them to remove any extra starch.

Bring a pot of water to a boil over medium heat, then drop in the water chestnuts. Stir gently to prevent them from sticking together or to the bottom of the pot. Boil for 3 to 5 minutes, or until the rubies float to the top. Transfer them to a bowl of ice-cold water and let soak for about 5 minutes. Then, drain well and transfer to a clean bowl. Add the remaining tablespoon (13 g) of sugar and mix well. Allow the rubies to rest in the sugar for at least 1 hour.

To make the pandan jelly, in a blender, blend the chopped pandan leaves with 1 cup (240 ml) of the water. Next, put the mixture in a piece of cheesecloth and squeeze it over a small bowl to get the pandan juice. In a pot off the heat, combine the remaining 1⅓ cups (320 ml) of water with the agar-agar powder and let soak for at least 15 minutes. Then, cook the agar-agar mixture over medium heat until hot.

In a small bowl, combine the jelly powder with the sugar and salt. Slowly sprinkle the jelly powder mixture into the pot and stir constantly until it is well combined without any lumps. Lower the heat to medium-low and let it simmer for another 1 to 2 minutes before removing from the heat. Finally, whisk in the prepared pandan leaf juice. Pour the jelly mixture into a 7-inch (18-cm) square cake pan and set aside to cool. Chill it in the fridge for about 1 hour, then unmold and cut into long strips or small cubes before serving.

To make the coconut milk soup, in a small bowl, combine the coconut milk, milk and condensed milk. Peel the longan fruits and remove the seeds. Tear the jackfruit meat into long strips. Remove the durian seeds. Place the pandan jelly, red rubies and fruits in a dessert glass or bowl, top with shaved ice and pour in the coconut milk soup to serve.

Sticky Rice Balls in Ginger Syrup (Che Troi Nuoc)

Yield:
6 servings

Che troi nuoc, meaning "sticky balls floating over water sweet soup," is a well-known dessert from South Vietnam, made of glutinous rice flour filled with yellow mung bean paste and served with a creamy coconut milk sauce and ginger syrup. Aside from the large filled rice balls, it also includes small unfilled rice balls called *che y*. The dessert gets its name from the fact that the sticky rice balls are boiled in water and float on the surface when cooked. It has a beautiful appearance and a sweet aroma, complemented by the warm and spicy flavor of ginger syrup and the nutty taste of roasted sesame. Adding the optional fried shallots to the mung bean filling imparts a special scent that enhances the flavor and makes it more appealing.

Mung Bean Filling

4 oz (115 g) peeled split mung beans, soaked in water for 4 hours, then drained

2 cups (475 ml) water

Pinch of salt

3 tbsp (39 g) granulated sugar

¼ cup (60 ml) canned coconut milk

1 tbsp (15 ml) coconut oil

2 tbsp (20 g) fried shallot (optional)

Skin Dough

5 oz (140 g) potato, peeled and cooked

1 tbsp (13 g) granulated sugar

¼ tsp salt

¼ cup (60 ml) water

2½ cups (300 g) glutinous rice flour

¾ cup (180 ml) boiling water

To make the filling, in a medium-sized saucepan, combine the drained mung beans with the water and salt. Bring to a boil over high heat, and skim off any white foam that forms on the surface. Then, lower the heat to medium-low, cover and let it simmer for 20 minutes, or until the beans become tender. Then, remove from the heat. Transfer the beans to a blender and blend with the granulated sugar and coconut milk until smooth.

Pass the mixture through a fine-mesh sieve into a medium-sized nonstick skillet and stir over low heat until it boils. Add half of the coconut oil at a time, mixing thoroughly after each addition. Finally, add the fried shallot (if using) and stir constantly for 7 to 10 minutes, or until the mixture gets thick and can be shaped like dough and maintain its shape.

Once done, remove from the heat, transfer to a heatproof container, cover with plastic wrap and let cool to room temperature. Once cooled, divide the filling into 20 equal-sized portions, about 1 level tablespoon (15 g) each. Roll them into smooth balls and cover with plastic wrap or a clean kitchen towel to prevent drying.

To make the dough, mash the cooked potato until smooth and, in a small bowl, combine it with the granulated sugar, salt and (room-temperature) water.

(continued)

Sticky Rice Balls in Ginger Syrup (Continued)

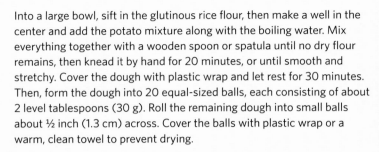

Ginger Syrup

1 oz (30 g) fresh ginger

1 qt (946 ml) water

1 lb (455 g) palm sugar, or to taste

⅓ tsp salt

5 pandan leaves (optional)

Coconut Milk Sauce (page 14), for serving

Toasted sesame seeds, for serving

Into a large bowl, sift in the glutinous rice flour, then make a well in the center and add the potato mixture along with the boiling water. Mix everything together with a wooden spoon or spatula until no dry flour remains, then knead it by hand for 20 minutes, or until smooth and stretchy. Cover the dough with plastic wrap and let rest for 30 minutes. Then, form the dough into 20 equal-sized balls, each consisting of about 2 level tablespoons (30 g). Roll the remaining dough into small balls about ½ inch (1.3 cm) across. Cover the balls with plastic wrap or a warm, clean towel to prevent drying.

Take out one large dough ball and flatten it with your palms into a 3-inch (7.5-cm) disk. Put a ball of the mung bean filling in the middle and pull the sides of the dough up to cover it. Roll it gently between your hands to make a smooth ball. Repeat with the remaining dough and filling.

Bring a large saucepan of water to a boil over high heat, then lower the heat to medium. Add the filled balls and small balls all at the same time, and cook for 10 to 15 minutes, or until they rise to the surface. Transfer the cooked balls to a bowl of cold water and let soak for 5 minutes before draining.

Make the ginger syrup by peeling the ginger and cutting into thin coins or strips. In a large saucepan, combine the water, palm sugar, salt and pandan leaves (if using). Bring to a boil over high heat, then remove the pandan leaves and add the ginger. Lower the heat to low and let the syrup simmer for 5 minutes. Add the cooked balls and simmer for another 5 minutes before serving.

To serve, place a few filled and a few small rice balls in a bowl and ladle some ginger syrup over them. Drizzle with coconut milk sauce, sprinkle with toasted sesame seeds and serve hot. For the best experience, it's recommended to consume this dessert on the day it was made. Putting it in the fridge overnight will make the dough harden and make the skin less tasty.

Pomelo Sweet Soup (Che Buoi)

Pomelo sweet soup is a delightful and simple dessert that originated in An Giang, a province in southwestern Vietnam. The main ingredient is pomelo pith, which is often overlooked, making this dessert cost-effective and easy to make. With careful preparation to remove the bitterness, the chewy pomelo pith and tender mung beans create a delicious sweet soup that is a popular item in sweet and dessert shops.

Pomelo Pearls

1 lb (455 g) pomelo peel

8 cups (1.9 L) water, divided

2 tbsp (36 g) salt

1 tsp alum powder (see page 153)

½ cup (60 g) + 3 tbsp (24 g) tapioca starch, divided

⅓ cup (67 g) granulated sugar

To make the pomelo pearls, remove the green skin from the pomelo peel, keeping the white pith. Ensure that there is no green skin left, as it will impart a bitter taste to the sweet soup. Cut the pith into ¼ x ¾-inch (0.5 x 2-cm) pieces and soak them in a mixture of 3 cups (720 ml) of water and salt for 5 to 6 hours.

After soaking, squeeze out the water and place the pomelo pith in a large bowl. Cover the pith with an inch or two (2.5 to 5 cm) of fresh water and squeeze it with your hands several times to extract the essential oil. Repeat this process five to ten times, or until the pomelo pith no longer tastes bitter.

In a small saucepan, combine 3 cups (720 ml) of fresh water and the alum powder, and bring to a boil over high heat. Add the pomelo pith and bring the water back to a boil. Remove the pith, rinse in cold water and squeeze out the excess water. In a large bowl, combine 2 cups (480 ml) of fresh water and 3 tablespoons (24 g) of the tapioca starch. Add the pith pieces and squeeze them a few times with your hands. Finally, gently squeeze the excess water out using your hands, being careful not to squeeze too tightly in order to keep the starch water inside the pith pieces.

In a medium-sized dry bowl, combine the pomelo pith and granulated sugar and mix well. Set aside for 15 to 20 minutes, or until the sugar dissolves. Heat a medium-sized nonstick skillet over low heat, then add the sugared pomelo pith and stir continuously until the sugar water evaporates. Turn off the heat when the pith is dry and transfer to a dry medium-sized bowl. Add the ½ cup (60 g) tapioca starch and stir well so that the starch coats all the pith pieces. Sift once to remove any excess starch.

To cook the pomelo pearls, bring a pot of water to a boil over medium-high heat. Add the pomelo pearls and cook them until they become transparent and rise to the surface, which should take a few minutes. Once cooked, remove from the heat and transfer them to a bowl of ice-cold water. Let soak for 5 minutes to cool down completely before draining.

(continued)

Pomelo Sweet Soup (Continued)

Sweet Soup

4 oz (115 g) peeled split mung beans, soaked in water for 4 hours, then drained

6 cups (1.4 L) + ¼ cup (60 ml) water, divided

4 oz (115 g) palm sugar

2 oz (60 g) rock sugar

Pinch of salt

⅓ cup (40 g) tapioca starch

Thick Coconut Sauce

2 cups (480 ml) canned coconut milk

3 tbsp (42 g) granulated sugar

Pinch of salt

2 tbsp (16 g) tapioca starch

Shaved ice, for serving (optional)

To make the sweet soup, prepare a steamer with about 3 inches (7.5 cm) of water and steam the mung beans for 20 minutes, until they become soft. In a large saucepan, combine the 6 cups (1.4 L) of water, palm sugar, rock sugar and salt, then bring to a boil over medium-high heat. Add the cooked pomelo pearls and mung beans to the pot and stir to combine. In a small bowl, mix the tapioca starch and remaining ¼ cup (60 ml) of water, then slowly add the mixture to the pot to thicken the soup. Cook the sweet soup for another minute before removing from the heat.

To make the thick coconut sauce, in a small saucepan, combine the coconut milk, sugar, salt and tapioca starch. Stir constantly over low heat for 2 to 3 minutes, or until it thickens, then remove from the heat.

The pomelo sweet soup can be served either hot or cold. For a warm dessert, scoop the sweet soup into a bowl or glass, drizzle the thick coconut sauce over it and serve immediately. If you prefer a cold dessert, you can also add shaved ice to the sweet soup, then mix well and enjoy. Any leftovers can be stored in an airtight container in the fridge for up to 2 days.

Refreshing Herbal Dessert Drink
(Che Sam Bo Luong)

Yield:
6 servings

This is a sweet and refreshing dessert that combines various natural ingredients that promote health, cool down the body and improve sleep quality on hot days. It originated in China and has been modified through the years to suit Vietnamese taste. The drink is a popular item on the menu of dessert shops in Vietnam, especially in the central and southern provinces due to the hot weather. Check out my guide to Vietnamese ingredients on page 150 for more info about where to buy some of these ingredients.

2 oz (60 g) coix seeds, soaked in water for 6 hours, then drained

2 oz (60 g) lotus root, peeled

8 cups (1.9 L) water

2 oz (60 g) dried lotus seeds, soaked in water for 1 hour, then drained

8 oz (225 g) rock sugar

4 oz (115 g) dried longans, soaked in water for 1 hour, then drained

1 oz (30 g) dried jujubes (red dates), soaked in water for 30 minutes, then drained

½ oz (15 g) dried shredded kelp, soaked in water for 30 minutes, then drained

1 oz (30 g) dried white seaweed, soaked in water for 30 minutes, then drained

½ oz (15 g) dried goji berries, soaked in water for 20 minutes, then drained

Shaved ice, for serving

Bring a small saucepan of water to a boil, then add the coix seeds and cook for about 15 minutes, or until soft. Then, drain the water and rinse the seeds with cold water to prevent them from clumping together.

Slice the peeled lotus root into ¼-inch (6-mm)-thick disks and rinse well. In a large saucepan, combine the lotus root and 8 cups (1.9 L) of water and heat over medium heat. Once the water boils, lower the heat to low and add the drained lotus seeds. Simmer for about 15 minutes, or until the lotus seeds are tender. Then, add the rock sugar and stir until it dissolves.

Next, add the drained dried longans and jujubes to the pot and cook for an additional 5 minutes. Finally, add the drained shredded kelp, white seaweed and goji berries, stir well and turn off the heat. Let cool completely at room temperature before refrigerating until serving.

To assemble the dessert, place the cooked coix seeds at the bottom of a dessert glass. Layer the other ingredients on top and finish with shaved ice. For the best flavor, serve cold. Any leftovers can be stored in an airtight container in the fridge for up to 2 days.

Rainbow Dessert (Che Suong Sa Hat Luu)

This dessert is a colorful and popular sweet in Vietnam. *Suong sa* is jelly made from konnyaku jelly powder, and *hat luu* are crunchy and chewy seeds made from water chestnuts shaped to look like pomegranate seeds, also called "rubies." The dish features a variety of colors, including yellow mung bean paste, crunchy rubies, clear white jelly and milky coconut milk sauce. When consumed, it provides a refreshing and sweet taste that is perfect for hot days.

Mung Bean Paste

4 oz (115 g) peeled split mung beans, soaked in water for 4 hours, then drained

2 cups (475 ml) water

Pinch of salt

¼ cup (50 g) sugar

½ cup (120 ml) canned coconut milk

Three-Colored Rubies

1 oz (30 g) chopped pandan leaves, or 5 drops green food coloring

1½ cups (355 ml) water, for coloring, divided

2 oz (60 g) peeled carrot, or 5 drops yellow food coloring

2 oz (60 g) peeled beet, or 5 drops red food coloring

12 oz (345 g) water chestnuts, peeled and diced

1½ cups (180 g) tapioca starch, divided

6 cups (1.4 L) water, for cooking, divided

6 tbsp (78 g) sugar, divided

To make the mung bean paste, in a small saucepan, combine the drained mung beans, water and salt and bring to a boil over medium heat, skimming off any white foam that forms on the surface. Then, lower the heat to medium-low, cover and let simmer for 20 minutes, or until the beans become tender. Remove from the heat and, in a blender, blend the cooked beans and cooking water with the sugar and coconut milk until smooth.

Pass the mixture through a fine-mesh sieve into a medium-sized nonstick skillet and cook over medium-low heat for around 5 minutes, or until thickened to a pastelike consistency. Remove the pan from the heat and transfer the mung bean paste to a small bowl. Cover the bowl with plastic wrap to prevent drying, and let cool to room temperature. Store the paste in the fridge until ready to use.

To create three-colored rubies, begin by making natural dyes for the water chestnuts. In a blender, blend the chopped pandan leaves with ½ cup (120 ml) of the water, then strain the mixture into a small bowl to extract the juice. Rinse the blender to remove the color. Cut the carrot into small pieces and blend with ½ cup (120 ml) of the remaining water, then strain the mixture into a separate small bowl. The beet juice can be prepared in the same way as the carrot juice; rinse the blender again before using. Alternatively, use food coloring by, in separate bowls, mixing green, yellow and red food coloring with ½ cup (120 ml) of water per bowl.

Divide the diced water chestnuts into three equal-sized portions and soak one portion per bowl in the prepared colored water for 15 minutes. After soaking, drain the water chestnuts, reserving the soaking liquid in separate clean bowls. Next, mix ½ cup (60 g) of the tapioca starch with each separate colored portion of the water chestnuts to coat them evenly. Finally, sift each portion of the water chestnuts to remove any extra starch.

(continued)

Rainbow Dessert (Continued)

Coconut Jelly

1 tbsp (9 g) agar-agar powder

3 cups (710 ml) coconut water

3 tbsp (39 g) sugar

Pinch of salt

Shaved ice, for serving

Coconut Milk Sauce (page 14), for serving

In a medium-sized saucepan, bring 2 cups (475 ml) of the fresh water and the reserved green soaking liquid to a boil over medium-high heat. Add the green rubies and stir to prevent sticking. Boil for 3 to 5 minutes, or until they float to the top, then transfer them to a bowl of ice-cold water and let soak for 5 minutes. Drain and transfer to a clean bowl; add 2 tablespoons (26 g) of the sugar and let soak for at least 1 hour. Repeat the process to separately cook the yellow and red rubies in their respective reserved soaking liquid, sugaring and letting them cool in separate bowls.

To make the coconut jelly, in a small saucepan off the heat, combine the agar-agar powder and coconut water and let soak for around 30 minutes. Place over medium heat and stir the mixture until it comes to a boil. Lower the heat to medium-low, add the sugar and salt and let simmer for another 1 to 2 minutes before removing from the heat. Pour the jelly into a 7-inch (18-cm) square cake pan and place in the refrigerator to chill fully. Before serving, cut the jelly into small cubes or long strips as desired.

When ready to serve, arrange shaved ice in the bottom of a dessert glass, followed by layers of the colored rubies, coconut jelly and mung bean paste. Finally, drizzle with coconut milk sauce. For the best experience, it's recommended to consume this dessert on the day it was made. Storing the rubies in the fridge can cause them to harden and lose their chewy texture.

Sweet Potato, Taro and Cassava Sweet Soup
(Che Ba Ba)

A mixed sweet soup that is emblematic of South Vietnam, this dessert brings together a variety of easy-to-find, simple and inexpensive ingredients. Some people attribute the name *ba ba* to the dish's creator, while others believe it to be a reference to the typical attire of women in South Vietnam, known as *ao ba ba*, symbolizing its simplicity but uniqueness. This soup is widely loved and considered one of the tastiest desserts in Vietnam.

Cassava Pearls and Cubed Vegetables

8 oz (225 g) cassavas, peeled and soaked in water for 6 hours, then drained

½ oz (15 g) chopped pandan leaves

¼ cup (60 ml) water

1 rounded cup (130 g) tapioca starch, divided

2 tsp (9 g) granulated sugar

4 oz (115 g) sweet potato, peeled and cut into ½-inch (1.3-cm) cubes

4 oz (115 g) taro, peeled and cut into ½-inch (1.3-cm) cubes

4 oz (115 g) purple yam (ube), peeled and cut into ½-inch (1.3-cm) cubes

To make the cassava pearls, grate the cassavas to achieve a fine texture and remove the woody core. Put the grated cassava in a piece of cheesecloth and squeeze it over a small bowl to extract the liquid. Reserve the grated cassava. Set the liquid aside for 1 hour to allow the starch to settle. Afterward, pour off and discard the water above the settled starch.

In a blender, blend the chopped pandan leaves with the water until smooth. Next, put the mixture in a separate piece of cheesecloth and squeeze it over a separate small bowl to get the pandan juice. Measure out 3 tablespoons (45 ml) of the pandan juice to use in the recipe.

In a medium-sized bowl, combine the grated cassava, cassava starch, pandan juice, 5 tablespoons (38 g) of the tapioca starch and the sugar, and mix well. Form small pearls from the dough, approximately ⅜ inch (1 cm) in diameter. Coat them evenly with 3 tablespoons (23 g) of the tapioca starch.

Working in three batches divided by vegetable, in separate bowls, coat the sweet potato, taro and purple yam cubes with 3 tablespoons (23 g) of the remaining tapioca starch per batch. Sift to eliminate any extra starch.

Bring a medium-sized saucepan of water to a boil over medium-high heat and, working in batches, cook the cassava pearls and vegetable cubes until they float to the top, then transfer them to a large bowl of cold water to cool down completely before draining.

(continued)

Sweet Potato, Taro and Cassava Sweet Soup (Continued)

Sweet Soup

7 cups (1.7 L) water

4 oz (115 g) peanuts, soaked in water for 10 hours, then drained

2 oz (60 g) peeled split mung beans, soaked in water for 4 hours, then drained

8 oz (225 g) rock sugar

1 oz (30 g) sago, soaked in water for 2 hours, then drained

2 oz (60 g) dried cassava sticks, soaked in water for 2 hours, then drained

½ oz (15 g) dried shredded kelp, soaked in water for 30 minutes, then drained

2 cups (475 ml) canned coconut milk

In a large saucepan, combine the 7 cups (1.7 L) of fresh water and drained peanuts and simmer over medium-low heat for 1 to 1½ hours, or until softened, then add the drained mung beans and simmer for 15 minutes. Add the rock sugar and stir until dissolved. Add the cooked vegetable cubes and cassava pearls, drained sago and drained cassava sticks, and simmer for 10 minutes. Finally, add the drained kelp and coconut milk, stir well and cook for 3 minutes before turning off the heat.

This sweet soup can be served hot immediately after cooking, or chilled in the fridge before eating. If you have leftovers, store in an airtight container in the fridge and eat within 1 to 2 days. After cooling in the fridge for about a day, the soup may thicken and resemble pudding. Eating it that way is perfectly fine, and it is a common preference among many Vietnamese people I know. To enjoy this dessert as if it were freshly made, simply add a small amount of boiling water, heat in a saucepan over medium-high heat and adjust the sweetness with sugar to taste. Then, serve hot or cold, according to your preference.

Mung Bean with Aloe Vera Sweet Soup
(Che Dau Xanh Pho Tai Nha Dam)

Yield:
6 servings

This is a delightful dessert that holds a special place in Vietnamese cuisine for its ability to both refresh and promote good health. Made with mung beans, aloe vera and shredded kelp, this dessert offers effective cooling properties on hot days, as well as potential benefits for skin health and relaxation to help you sleep better.

4 oz (115 g) mung beans

½ oz (15 g) dried shredded kelp

10 oz (280 g) fresh aloe vera

2½ tsp (15 g) salt, divided

1 tbsp (15 ml) fresh lemon or lime juice

10 oz (280 g) rock sugar, divided

2 qt (1.9 L) water

1 tsp vanilla extract

Shaved ice, for serving (optional)

Rinse the mung beans thoroughly, then soak in water for 4 hours or overnight. If you're short on time, soak in warm water for 1 hour instead. Once soaked, rinse the beans with clean water and drain.

Soak the dried kelp in water for 30 minutes, or until softened, then rinse and drain.

In the meantime, cut the aloe vera into 4-inch (10-cm) lengths, then remove and discard the spines and outer green skin. Rinse, then slice them into thin strips. Put the strips in a medium-sized bowl and sprinkle 2 teaspoons (12 g) of the salt and the lemon juice over them. Squeeze the strips together gently with your hands, then rinse several times under running water to remove any slime or yellow gel.

Bring a medium-sized pot of water to a boil over high heat. Add the aloe vera strips and cook for 30 seconds. Then, transfer them to a bowl of ice-cold water and let soak for 5 minutes before transferring to another dry bowl. Add half of the rock sugar (5 ounces [140 g]) to the aloe vera and mix well, then let sit for 30 minutes to absorb the sugar.

To make the sweet soup, combine the drained mung beans, fresh water and remaining ½ teaspoon of salt in a medium-sized saucepan and bring to a boil over high heat. Skim off any white foam that forms on the surface, then lower the heat to medium-low and let simmer for 30 minutes, or until the beans are tender. Add the remaining 5 ounces (140 g) of rock sugar and dissolve it in the soup. Next, add the aloe vera and cook for 3 minutes. Add the vanilla and stir in the drained kelp. Finally, remove the pot from the heat.

This sweet soup can be enjoyed hot or cold with shaved ice. It can be stored in the refrigerator for up to 2 days.

3-Color Dessert (Che Ba Mau)

This dessert is a visually appealing sweet soup that features three colors: red, yellow and green, which come from red beans, mung beans and pandan jelly, respectively. This dish is not only popular, but also many Vietnamese people associate it with their childhood.

Yellow Layer (Mung Bean Paste)

4 oz (115 g) peeled split mung beans, soaked in water for 4 hours, then drained

2 cups (475 ml) water

Pinch of salt

¼ cup (50 g) sugar

½ cup (120 ml) canned coconut milk

Green Layer (Pandan Jelly)

1.5 oz (40 g) chopped pandan leaves

3 cups (710 ml) water, divided

1 tbsp (9 g) agar-agar powder

3 tbsp (39 g) sugar

Pinch of salt

Red Layer (Sweet Kidney Beans)

4 oz (115 g) dried kidney beans or red beans, soaked in water for 6 hours, then drained, or 1 (12-oz [340-g]) can, drained and rinsed

2 cups (475 ml) water

¼ tsp salt

3 tbsp (39 g) sugar

Shaved ice, for serving

Coconut Milk Sauce (page 14), for serving

To make the yellow layer, in a small saucepan, combine the drained mung beans, water and salt, and bring to a boil over medium heat, skimming off any white foam. Then, lower the heat to medium-low, cover and let simmer for 20 minutes, or until the beans become tender. Then, remove from the heat. In a blender, blend the cooked beans and cooking water with the sugar and coconut milk until smooth.

Pass the mixture through a fine-mesh sieve into a medium-sized nonstick skillet. Cook over medium-low heat for around 5 minutes, or until thickened to a pastelike consistency. Remove from the heat and transfer to a small bowl. Cover the bowl with plastic wrap to prevent drying, and let the paste cool to room temperature. Store the paste in the fridge.

To make the green layer, in a blender, blend the chopped pandan leaves with 2 cups (470 ml) of the water. Next, put the mixture in a piece of cheesecloth or nut milk bag and squeeze it over a small bowl to get the pandan juice. In a medium-sized saucepan off the heat, combine the remaining cup (240 ml) of water with the agar-agar powder and soak for around 30 minutes. Then, over medium heat, cook the agar-agar mixture until it comes to a boil. Lower the heat to medium-low, add the sugar and salt and let simmer for another 1 to 2 minutes before removing from the heat. Finally, add the pandan juice and stir well to combine. Pour the jelly mixture into a 7-inch (18-cm) square cake pan and set aside to cool. Put it in the fridge for about 1 hour, then unmold and cut into small cubes or long strips before serving.

If using dried kidney beans to make the red layer, in a medium-sized saucepan, combine the beans, water and salt. Bring to a boil over high heat, and skim off any white foam that forms on the surface. Then, lower the heat to medium-low and simmer for 1½ to 2 hours, or until the beans are soft and tender. Drain the beans and transfer them to a small saucepan along with the sugar. Stir over medium-low heat for 7 to 10 minutes to help the sugar dissolve and soak into the beans. If using canned red beans, drain and rinse, then stir in the sugar as described above.

When you are ready to serve, put each layer in the dessert glass, top with shaved ice and drizzle with coconut milk sauce. You can store each layer separately in the fridge for up to 2 days.

Clear Tapioca Balls with Roasted Pork Filling Sweet Soup (Che Bot Loc Boc Heo Quay)

Yield:
6 servings

This is a specialty dessert from Hue, Vietnam, traditionally served only to kings in the imperial court. It is a sweet soup made of tapioca pearls filled with roasted pork, which may seem like an unusual combination, but the skillful preparation creates a harmonious balance of flavors. It is a must-try when visiting Hue.

7 oz (200 g) roasted pork belly, cut into very tiny pieces

⅓ cup (67 g) granulated sugar

2 dried wood-ear mushrooms, soaked in warm water for 1 to 2 hours, drained and thoroughly rinsed

½ tsp salt

1½ cups (180 g) tapioca starch

⅓ cup (80 ml) boiling water

1 qt (946 ml) water

5 pandan leaves (optional)

9 oz (255 g) rock sugar

Shaved ice, for serving (optional)

Place the roasted pork in a pot of boiling water for 5 minutes to remove any charred taste or strong spices. Remove and drain the pork and place it in a clean bowl. Mix in the granulated sugar and set aside for about 30 minutes. Next, cut the hard stem off of the wood-ear mushrooms and slice them into thin fibers.

Heat a medium-sized nonstick skillet, add the pork and sauté for about 15 minutes, until the pork fat melts. Remove and discard the extra fat before adding the wood-ear mushroom fibers and salt, then stir-fry for 10 minutes until the mushrooms are cooked and the mixture is dry. Remove the pan from the heat and set aside to cool.

Place the tapioca starch in a small bowl. Slowly pour the boiling water into the center of the bowl while stirring with a wooden spoon until all the starch is incorporated. Use your hands to knead the dough until it becomes smooth, elastic and no longer sticky. Divide the dough into four equal-sized pieces and roll each into a 1-inch (2.5-cm)-thick strand. Cut these strands into ½-inch (1.3-cm) pieces. Roll each piece into a ball, then flatten it. Put ½ teaspoon of the pork onto the center of the dough. Wrap the dough around the filling and gently shape it into a ball, then repeat to create multiple balls.

Bring a medium-sized saucepan of water to a boil, add the tapioca balls and cook for 30 minutes over medium-low heat. When the skin becomes transparent and floats to the surface, they are cooked. Transfer them to a bowl of cold water to keep them from sticking together.

Pour fresh water into a medium-sized saucepan and add the pandan leaves (if using), bring to a boil over high heat, then remove the pandan leaves. Stir the rock sugar into the water until it dissolves. Add the tapioca balls to the pot and continue to cook for 10 minutes before turning off the heat.

Spoon the tapioca balls and sugar syrup into a dessert glass; you may enjoy it hot or cold with shaved ice. This sweet soup is best eaten on the day it was made. Putting it in the fridge overnight will make the dough harden and make the skin less tasty.

Pretty and Elegant Sweets

The first half of this chapter explores the fascinating fusion of classic Vietnamese tastes with culinary inspirations from around the world. One delicious example of this blend of Western and Vietnamese cuisine can be found in dishes like Crème Caramel (page 79) paired with coffee, cheesecake featuring tangy passion fruit (page 81) or crepes stuffed with the uniquely flavored durian fruit (page 85), which is the most popular fruit in Southeast Asia. In addition to these sweet treats, Vietnamese bakers have also created savory versions of sponge cake (see Salted Egg Yolk Savory Cake, page 86, for mine) topped with their own sauces and toppings, which are hugely popular and often sell out in local bakeries.

The remaining recipes are my creations, inspired by the refreshing and sweet desserts that are popular among young people in Vietnam. For instance, I have a recipe for delicious Pineapple Cookie Rolls (page 89) that draws inspiration from the Malaysian pineapple tart. The cookie rolls are decorated with adorable little bear faces that add a touch of playfulness to the dish. Additionally, I have included modern sweet soups called che in my recipe collection. These include Milk Pudding and Lychee Sweet Gruel (page 92), Coconut Jelly with Coconut Pearls Dessert (page 95) and many more. All of these desserts are not only delicious but also very attractive with their varied textures, sweet flavors and colorful appearance. I hope that my recipes will inspire you to try making these che dishes at home, so that you can experience the diverse and wonderful food culture of Vietnam.

Crème Caramel (Banh Flan)

Yield:
4 pieces

This dessert—also known as caramel pudding, condensed milk pudding or caramel custard—consists of two main parts: a caramel layer and a custard made from eggs and milk. Originating from European cuisine and brought to Vietnam by the French during the colonial period, flan has become popular and loved by all ages in Vietnam. Vietnamese people often enjoy flan with coffee and shaved ice, sometimes combined with Coconut Milk Sauce (page 14) to increase creaminess. As a result, it has become an indispensable dessert in beverage and dessert shops from budget to high-end.

Caramel

½ cup (100 g) sugar

6 tbsp (90 ml) water, divided

Custard

4 large eggs

2 large egg yolks

1 tsp vanilla extract

1¾ cups (420 ml) milk

⅔ cup (160 ml) sweetened condensed milk

Shaved ice, for serving (optional)

Brewed coffee, for serving (optional)

Dark and white chocolate buttons (optional)

Gather four ovenproof molds, such as Pyrex® cups or ceramic ramekins, for the crème caramel. This recipe requires four molds each with a volume of 210 milliliters (a little under 1 cup).

To make the caramel, in a saucepan, combine the sugar and 3 tablespoons (45 ml) of the water and bring to a boil over medium heat. Turn the saucepan a few times to let the sugar absorb the water, but do not stir, to avoid crystallization. Heat the sugar until it turns golden-brown. Then, lower the heat to low, carefully pour in the remaining 3 tablespoons (45 ml) of water, and stir until the water and caramel sugar mix together. Wait about 10 seconds more, then remove from the heat and pour equal-sized amounts of the caramel into the four molds. Tilt the molds to spread the caramel evenly.

Preheat the oven to 300°F (150°C).

To make the custard, in a medium-sized bowl, whisk together the eggs, egg yolks and vanilla, being careful not to create air bubbles, which could cause holes to appear in the cake after baking.

In a small saucepan, whisk the milk and condensed milk together well over medium heat. Remove from the heat when it starts to steam. Pour the milk mixture slowly into the egg mixture, stirring constantly. Sieve the mixture to remove any lumps.

Pour the custard mixture through a sieve again and divide it equally among the caramel-filled molds. Place the molds in a deep baking pan and cover them with foil. Put the pan in the oven and fill it halfway with boiling water to ensure the custard bakes evenly.

(continued)

Crème Caramel (Continued)

Bake for 50 to 60 minutes, or until the custard is almost set. When the custards are done, they should jiggle slightly in the center.

Remove from the oven and let them cool down completely. Put them in the fridge for at least 2 hours to bring out the best flavor. Crème caramel lasts 5 to 7 days in the fridge.

To remove the crème caramel from the mold, run a knife along the edges, cover with a plate, then flip to enable it to come out. You may eat the crème caramel as is, or with shaved ice and coffee drizzled on top, as many Vietnamese do.

As you can see from the previous page's illustrations, I'm a big fan of cute bears! If you want to make your own bear-themed crème caramel, follow these steps to prepare melted chocolate: Place the dark chocolate buttons in a piping bag and securely tie it up. Do the same for the white chocolate. Soak the bags in a bowl of hot water for about a minute, or until the chocolate melts. After that, use the dark chocolate to draw the eyes and mouth, and white chocolate to draw the nose on top of your finished crème caramel. Don't forget to add unmelted chocolate buttons to create the bear ears! I'm confident that your loved ones will enjoy these adorable crème caramel treats.

No-Bake Passion Fruit Cheesecake
(Banh Pho Mai Chanh Day)

Yield:
6 servings

Passion fruit has given Western cheesecake a tropical twist in Vietnam, resulting in this popular no-bake version that's often served at birthday parties. This dessert has a biscuit base, a sweet and creamy cheesecake layer and a sweet-and-sour passion fruit jelly topping, creating a perfectly balanced flavor. If you're a cheesecake lover looking to add another delicious cake to your culinary collection, you should definitely try this recipe.

Base

4 oz (115 g) digestive biscuits or graham crackers

¼ cup (55 g) unsalted butter, melted

Cheesecake Filling

¼ cup (60 ml) cold water

1 tbsp (9 g) powdered gelatin

2 passion fruits

3 tbsp (45 ml) hot water

9 oz (255 g) cream cheese, at room temperature

½ cup (100 g) sugar

1 cup (240 ml) heavy cream

Have ready a 6-inch (15-cm) mousse ring or springform pan. If using a mousse ring, secure the bottom with several layers of plastic wrap.

To make the base, use a blender or food processor to blend the biscuits into fine crumbs, then place in a small bowl and mix them well with the melted butter. Transfer the mixture to the mold and use a glass or spatula to press it tightly into an even layer on the bottom. Chill in the fridge until needed.

Prepare the filling by placing the cold water in a small bowl, sprinkling the powdered gelatin into it and stirring well. Set aside for about 5 minutes to allow the gelatin to bloom. Then, dissolve the gelatin by putting the bowl in a larger bowl of hot water and stirring until it is completely melted, or by heating it in a microwave on low for about 10 seconds.

Cut the passion fruits in half, scoop the pulp into a cup and mix with the hot water. Strain the mixture through a sieve into a small bowl to remove the seeds.

In a medium-sized bowl, cream together the cream cheese and sugar until smooth. Then, add the melted gelatin and passion fruit juice and stir until well combined.

In a large cold, clean bowl, whip the cream until it thickens and forms soft peaks. Pour a third of the whipped cream into the cream cheese mixture, fold until fully mixed, then add the remaining whipped cream and continue to fold until well combined. Pour the cheesecake filling onto the prepared base and spread it evenly to make a smooth surface. Place the cake in the fridge for 1 hour, or until the surface has set.

(continued)

No-Bake Passion Fruit Cheesecake (Continued)

Passion Fruit Jelly

2 passion fruits

3 tbsp (45 ml) hot water

3 tbsp (39 g) sugar

2 tsp (6 g) powdered gelatin

3 tbsp (45 ml) cold water

To make the passion fruit jelly, follow the earlier directions to extract the juice of the 2 passion fruits. Reserve about 1 teaspoon of the seeds for garnish, if desired. In a small bowl, mix the passion fruit juice and sugar together until all the sugar is dissolved. Use the same method as before to bloom and melt the powdered gelatin while you are making the juice. After the gelatin has melted, add it to the passion fruit mixture and give it a thorough swirl. Let the mixture cool completely.

Finally, pour the jelly mixture over the cheesecake and add the reserved passion fruit seeds as a garnish, if desired. Return the cheesecake to the fridge and let chill until the cheesecake is fully set, 4 to 5 hours.

There are a couple of ways to remove the cheesecake from the pan. One option is to use a hair dryer and direct the heat from about 5 inches (13 cm) away onto the edges of the pan. This will soften the edges of the cheesecake, making it easier to remove and giving it a smooth edge. Another option is to wrap a warm towel around the pan, which will have the same effect.

The passion fruit cheesecake will look beautiful once finished, but to make it even more visually appealing, you could consider adding fresh fruit toppings, whipped cream frosting or edible flowers. For optimal freshness, consume within 3 days when stored in the fridge.

Durian Crepes (Banh Crepe Sau Rieng)

Yield: 7 to 8 crepes

Durian is known as the "king of fruits" in Southeast Asia due to its fragrant sweetness that captivates many people. One popular dessert in Vietnam that incorporates durian is crepes with whipped cream and durian flesh filling. In contrast to crepes in other places that may be slightly scorched, Vietnamese bakers prioritize creating a smooth and glossy surface. The soft crepe layer combined with the rich and creamy filling of durian flesh creates an unforgettable flavor that doesn't require any additional toppings.

Crepes

½ cup (65 g) all-purpose flour

1 tbsp (8 g) cornstarch

1 tbsp (8 g) powdered sugar

1 large egg

¾ cup (180 ml) milk

⅓ cup (80 ml) canned coconut milk

1 or 2 drops yellow food coloring (optional)

Neutral oil, for pan

Durian Filling

8 oz (225 g) durian flesh (seedless)

1 cup (240 ml) heavy cream

1 tbsp (13 g) granulated sugar

Dark and white chocolate buttons (optional)

To make the crepes, in a medium-sized bowl, sift together the flour, cornstarch and powdered sugar. In a small bowl, whisk together the egg, milk and coconut milk. Pour the egg mixture into the flour mixture and stir constantly until well incorporated. Sieve the mixture to eliminate lumps. If desired, add 1 or 2 drops of yellow food coloring to enhance the color of the crepes. Cover the bowl with plastic wrap and refrigerate the batter for an hour.

Heat a medium-sized nonstick skillet over medium heat, then lower the heat to very low and brush a thin layer of oil over the pan. Pour about ¼ cup (60 ml) of the batter into the pan and tilt the pan in a circle to spread out the batter. Fry for 60 to 90 seconds, or until the crepe is dry and air bubbles are visible below. Allow the crepe to cool on parchment paper. Continue to fry the remaining crepes, one at a time.

To make the durian filling, mash the durian flesh with a fork, place in a small bowl and keep it cold until you need it. In addition to durian, you may use other fruits, such as mango, kiwi or strawberry.

In a dry, clean bowl, chilled if possible, combine the cream and granulated sugar. Whip with a whisk or electric mixer until it thickens and forms firm peaks. To make it easier to inject the filling into the crepes, transfer the whipped cream to a piping bag.

Spread out a crepe on a flat surface, inject it with the sweetened whipped cream and put some durian flesh in the middle. Tightly fold the crepe into quarters around the filling. Before serving, allow the crepes to chill in the refrigerator for 1 to 2 hours. This will ensure that they have the best taste.

To create the cute bear face on the crepes, simply follow the instructions on page 80 for melting chocolate buttons and use them to decorate the bear face as shown. I hope you and your loved ones enjoy this adorable durian crepe variation!

Salted Egg Yolk Savory Cake
(Banh Bong Lan Trung Muoi)

**Yield:
3 servings**

Salted egg sponge cake is a popular cake in Vietnam that combines soft and fluffy sponge cake with savory meat floss and special sauces. It's always a top choice for Vietnamese people when they want to satisfy their cake cravings. A key component of the cake is the special sauce called *sot dau trung* (oil-egg sauce), which has a similar method to making mayonnaise but has a transparent, golden appearance. If you visit Vietnam and don't try salted egg sponge cake, you're definitely missing out.

Sponge Cake

6 large eggs, separated

1 tsp vanilla extract

¼ cup (60 ml) lukewarm milk (about 105°F [40°C])

¼ cup (60 ml) neutral oil or melted unsalted butter

¾ cup + 1 tbsp (100 g) cake flour

½ tsp fresh lemon juice or rice vinegar

½ cup (100 g) sugar

To make the sponge cake, line the bottom of a 10½ x 15-inch (27 x 38-cm) rectangular cake pan with parchment paper and preheat the oven to 340°F (170°C).

In a medium-sized bowl, mix together the 6 egg yolks and vanilla. Then, stir in the milk and oil to fully incorporate. Sift in the cake flour and mix until a smooth batter forms with no dry flour clumps.

In a separate large bowl, using an electric mixer, beat the 6 egg whites and lemon juice on low speed until foamy. Gradually add the sugar in three parts, beating for 30 to 45 seconds after each addition until the sugar is dissolved. Continue to beat until the mixture forms stiff peaks with tips that fall in a hooklike shape.

Gently fold in one-third of the beaten egg whites into the egg yolk batter. Then, pour this back into the rest of the whites and gently fold together with a spatula until everything is well mixed. It's important to not overmix the batter, as doing so could cause the air bubbles to burst and result in a poorly risen and potentially fallen sponge cake.

Finally, pour the batter into the prepared pan. The batter should have a ribbonlike appearance if mixed correctly. Gently smooth the top of the batter and tap the pan on a flat surface a few times to release any large air bubbles. Bake for 30 to 35 minutes on the second rack from the bottom. Once the cake is finished and the top has turned golden, immediately remove it from the oven and turn it out of the pan. Discard the parchment paper and let the cake cool completely.

(continued)

Salted Egg Yolk Savory Cake (Continued)

Oil-Egg Sauce

2 large egg yolks

1 tbsp (13 g) sugar

¼ tsp salt

¼ tsp fresh lemon or lime juice

1¼ cups (300 ml) neutral oil

Cream Cheese Sauce

4 oz (115 g) cream cheese, at room temperature

2 tbsp (26 g) sugar

1 tbsp (8 g) cornstarch

⅓ cup (80 ml) milk

⅓ cup (80 ml) heavy cream

2 tbsp (28 g) unsalted butter

Toppings

6 salted egg yolks, cooked (see page 150)

½ cup (60 g) pork or chicken floss (see page 151)

3 creamy cheese wedges (Laughing Cow® cheese wedges are mainly used in Vietnam)

To make the oil-egg sauce, in a medium-sized bowl, mix together the egg yolks, sugar, salt and lemon juice. Using a whisk, beat the ingredients until they form a pale-yellow mixture. Slowly pour in the oil while constantly whisking, making sure that each addition is fully mixed in. Keep whisking until the sauce thickens, gets shiny and almost becomes a translucent yellow color. To make decorating the cake simpler, transfer the sauce to a piping bag. You can store the sauce in the fridge for up to a week, avoiding the coldest section to prevent oil separation.

To make the cream cheese sauce, in a separate medium-sized bowl, stir together the cream cheese and sugar until smooth. Stir in the cornstarch, followed by the milk and cream, and continue to stir until fully incorporated. Pass the mixture through a sieve into a medium-sized saucepan. Cook over medium-low heat, stirring constantly, until the mixture thickens into a paste. Remove from the heat and stir in the unsalted butter until it melts and is well absorbed. Allow the sauce to cool before transferring it to a piping bag. It can be stored in the fridge for up to 3 days.

To assemble the cake, prepare the salted egg yolks: Quarter three of them and crush the other three. Then, slice the sponge cake into six equal-sized rectangular pieces and place one portion on an individual serving plate. Drizzle both the oil-egg sauce and cream cheese sauce over the cake in a crisscross pattern, then sprinkle with the crushed salted egg yolk and meat floss. Place a second layer of cake on top, followed by a drizzle of each sauce and some pork floss, the salted egg quarters and the cheese wedges. Repeat to assemble the other servings of cake.

The assembled cake can be kept at room temperature for up to 12 hours, or stored in the refrigerator for up to 3 days, ensuring freshness by keeping them in an airtight container.

Pineapple Cookie Rolls (Banh Dua)

Yield: 38 to 40 cookies

My inspiration for creating pineapple cookie rolls comes from the beloved pineapple tart, a sweet treat that originated from the fusion of Chinese and Malay cultures in the Malay Peninsula of Southeast Asia. These cookie rolls have a tender, melt-in-the-mouth texture that's rich with buttery goodness, similar to the tart crust that was introduced by Portuguese immigrants. Inside, you'll find a sticky, fragrant sweet-and-sour pineapple jam infused with cinnamon. This delectable snack is a favorite among the Vietnamese, who not only enjoy it as a treat while sipping tea and chatting, but also consider it a meaningful gift to give to friends and loved ones.

Pineapple Filling

1 lb (455 g) pineapple

3 oz (85 g) rock sugar

¼ tsp salt

2 tbsp (30 ml) light corn syrup or maltose

¼ tsp ground cinnamon

1½ tsp (7 g) unsalted butter

Crust

½ cup (1 stick, 114 g) unsalted butter, at room temperature

½ cup (60 g) powdered sugar

1 large egg yolk

2 tbsp (30 ml) heavy cream

1½ cups (185 g) all-purpose flour

¼ cup (30 g) milk powder

To make the pineapple filling, you have two options for preparing the pineapple. Grating the pineapple gives you the clear texture of the fibers when eating. Alternatively, you can grind the pineapple for a quicker process, but this method may limit the texture. In a medium-sized bowl, combine the grated or ground pineapple, rock sugar and salt. Let the sugar dissolve for 10 to 15 minutes.

Simmer the pineapple mixture in a medium-sized nonstick skillet over medium-high heat until the liquid has evaporated. Stir in the corn syrup and ground cinnamon until well combined. Cook over low heat until the mixture is golden brown and sticky, then add the butter and mix until melted and well absorbed into the filling. Remove from the heat and let the filling cool down.

Weigh the cooled filling and divide it into five equal-sized portions. Wrap each filling portion in plastic wrap and roll it up to make rolls that are about 6 inches (15 cm) long. Chill the rolls in the refrigerator for about 30 minutes while you prepare the crust.

To make the crust, in a large bowl using an electric mixer, beat the butter at low speed until smooth. Then, add the powdered sugar and beat until the mixture turns pale yellow. Add the egg yolk and cream to the bowl and keep beating until well combined.

Sift the flour and milk powder into the bowl and mix with a spatula until the dough comes together. Form it into a block, wrap with plastic wrap and chill in the freezer for 30 minutes to make it easier to roll and shape.

(continued)

Pineapple Cookie Rolls (Continued)

Egg Wash

1 large egg yolk

1½ tsp (7 ml) milk

Dark and white chocolate buttons (optional)

Divide the dough into five equal-sized portions. Roll out each portion of dough into a rectangle, ensuring it is 6 inches (15 cm) long and wide enough to cover the pineapple filling. Place a roll of pineapple filling on one edge of the dough, roll up the dough around it and then smooth out the seams. Repeat to create five filled rolls of dough. Form small balls with a little bit of the dough to resemble the bear's ears, if desired. Wrap the rolls in plastic wrap, reserving the ears separately in plastic wrap, and put them in the freezer for 20 to 30 minutes to harden, making them easier to cut.

Meanwhile, preheat the oven to 355°F (180°C) and line a baking sheet with parchment paper.

Cut the pineapple rolls into 1-inch (2.5-cm) pieces and place them on the prepared baking sheet. In a bowl, stir together the egg yolk and milk and use a pastry brush to gently glaze the rolls. Attach the dough ears to the top if making bear-shaped rolls.

Bake for 20 to 25 minutes on the second rack from the bottom, until the rolls turn light yellow and are evenly browned on top. After removing the rolls from the oven, allow them to cool. They may darken slightly as they cool.

Once the pineapple cookie rolls are cool, they can be enjoyed immediately or stored in the fridge for a day for optimal flavor. Any leftovers can be kept fresh for up to 3 to 4 days at room temperature in an airtight container, or for 7 to 10 days in the fridge.

If you've fallen in love with the adorable bear decorations and have made pineapple cookie rolls with bear ears as I have, take them to the next level by adding a cute bear face and nose with melted chocolate. Simply refer to the instructions for melting chocolate buttons on page 80 to create your own. Have fun decorating your own adorable bear pineapple cookie rolls!

Milk Pudding and Lychee Sweet Gruel
(Che Khuc Bach)

Yield:
6 servings

Che khuc bach is a beloved modern sweet soup and dessert in Vietnam. It features a milky cream pudding with a texture similar to panna cotta, which is served with a refreshing sugar syrup and fruits such as lychee, longan and jackfruit. It is finished off with crispy toasted almond slices on top for added texture. People of all ages enjoy this dessert, especially on hot days.

White Pudding

¼ cup (60 ml) cold water

1 tbsp (9 g) powdered gelatin

½ cup (120 ml) milk

½ cup (120 ml) heavy cream

3 tbsp (39 g) granulated sugar

1 tsp vanilla extract

Blue Pudding

¼ cup (60 ml) cold water

1 tbsp (9 g) powdered gelatin

½ cup (120 ml) milk

½ cup (120 ml) heavy cream

3 tbsp (39 g) granulated sugar

20 to 30 dried butterfly pea flowers (optional)

1 tsp vanilla extract

Lychee Sweet Soup

1 qt (946 ml) water

4 oz (115 g) rock sugar

5 pandan leaves (optional)

30 lychees, peeled and seeded

Shaved ice, for serving

Torn jackfruit flesh, for serving

Soaked chia seeds, for serving

Toasted sliced almonds, for serving

To make the white pudding, first pour the cold water into a small bowl, sprinkle with the powdered gelatin and stir well. Allow the gelatin to bloom for 5 minutes. In a small saucepan, combine the milk, cream and granulated sugar. Stir the mixture over medium-low heat to dissolve the sugar. Remove from the heat when it starts to steam. Add the bloomed gelatin and vanilla, and stir well.

Pour the pudding mixture through a fine-mesh sieve into a heatproof food container and refrigerate for at least 4 hours until fully chilled. The pudding can be stored in the fridge for up to 3 days.

To make the blue pudding, follow the same method as above. If using dried butterfly pea flowers, add them to the milk and cream mixture. Once the mixture turns blue, remove the flowers and continue with the remaining steps. In addition to using blue, you have the flexibility to use any color of your preference to dye the pudding. You may use natural colors derived from jams or powders or any food coloring of your choice.

To make the lychee sweet soup, in a medium-sized saucepan, combine the water, rock sugar and pandan leaves (if using). Cook over medium heat until the sugar dissolves and the mixture boils. Remove the pandan leaves and turn off the heat. Add the lychees to the mixture, let it cool to room temperature and chill in the fridge for at least an hour before serving.

To assemble the dessert, start by filling a dessert bowl half full with shaved ice. Cut the milk pudding into bite-sized pieces and place them on top of the ice, followed by the jackfruit, lychees (removed from the soup) and soaked chia seeds. Next, ladle the sweet soup on top and sprinkle with toasted sliced almonds.

Coconut Jelly with Coconut Pearls Dessert
(Che Dua Dam)

Yield:
6 servings

This coconut dessert originated in a dessert shop in Hai Phong, a northern province of Vietnam, and quickly became a favorite dessert of people all over the country. It is a harmonious combination of various coconut ingredients: fresh coconut water and coconut milk, chewy and crunchy pearls made from coconut meat and a creamy coconut milk sauce. If you love coconut, this dessert is sure to satisfy your craving.

Coconut and Coconut Milk Jellies

1 tbsp (9 g) konnyaku jelly powder (see page 150)

1 tbsp (13 g) granulated sugar

1 qt (946 ml) coconut water

3 oz (85 g) rock sugar

⅓ cup (80 ml) coconut milk

To make the coconut and coconut milk jellies, in a small bowl, mix together the konnyaku jelly powder and granulated sugar. In a large saucepan, combine the coconut water and rock sugar, and bring to a boil over medium-high heat. Slowly pour the jelly powder mixture into the coconut water while stirring, to keep the mixture from getting lumpy. Continue to heat the mixture for 2 minutes and then remove from the heat.

Pour half of the jelly mixture into a heatproof container. In a small bowl, combine the coconut milk with the remaining half of the jelly mixture, and pour the mixture through a sieve into a separate heatproof container. Allow the two mixtures to cool and firm up at room temperature before placing them in the fridge to chill until needed.

Cut the chilled coconut jelly into short strands or use a crinkle cutter to create a wavy pattern for a more visually appealing look. As for the coconut milk jelly, you can use a fruit peeler to create slices or simply use a knife to cut it into any desired shape.

(continued)

Coconut Jelly with Coconut Pearls Dessert (Continued)

Blue Coconut Pearls

⅓ cup (80 ml) water

3 tbsp (39 g) granulated sugar, divided

20 dried butterfly pea flowers, or blue food coloring

1 cup (120 g) + 1 tbsp (8 g) tapioca starch, divided, plus more if needed

4 oz (115 g) coconut meat, diced

Shaved ice, for serving

Young coconut meat, for serving

Coconut Milk Sauce (page 14), for serving

Toasted coconut flakes, for serving

To make the blue coconut pearls, in a small saucepan, bring the water, 2 tablespoons (26 g) of the granulated sugar and the dried butterfly pea flowers to a boil over medium-high heat. When the mixture becomes blue-purple, remove the flowers and turn off the heat. Pour the mixture into a bowl, add the cup (120 g) of tapioca starch and stir until the water is absorbed. Knead with your hands until you have a smooth, nonsticky dough. If your dough is still sticky, add some tapioca starch. If it's still dry, some hot water should do the trick.

Divide the dough into four or five equal-sized pieces, then roll each piece into a long rope about ½ inch (1.3 cm) in diameter. Cut the ropes into small pieces and roll each piece into a pearl about ½ inch (1.3 cm) in diameter. Flatten the pearl with your palm, put a piece of diced coconut meat in the middle, wrap it up carefully and roll it back into a pearl. Finally, evenly coat the pearls with the remaining tablespoon (8 g) of tapioca starch to keep them from sticking together.

Bring a medium-sized saucepan of water to a boil over medium-high heat, then add the pearls. Cook them for about 20 minutes, or until they float to the surface. Once the pearls have floated, turn off the heat, cover the pot and let them incubate for 30 minutes to thoroughly cook them. After that, transfer to a bowl of cold water to cool. Once cooled, drain the water and mix the pearls with the remaining tablespoon (13 g) of granulated sugar. Let the sugared pearls rest for 30 minutes before serving.

To assemble the dessert, start by filling a dessert bowl halfway with shaved ice. Arrange the jellies, pearls and young coconut meat on top of the ice. Drizzle coconut milk sauce over the top and sprinkle with toasted coconut flakes.

Avocado Pudding with Coconut Milk Sauce (Che Bo)

Yield:
6 servings

In Vietnam, avocado is often used to make many desserts and drinks, unlike in Western countries where it's typically used in salads and savory dishes. Some of the most famous avocado-based treats in Vietnam are avocado ice cream, avocado smoothies, avocado milk tea and *che bo*—a delightful combination of smooth and creamy avocado pudding, refreshing jelly, chewy avocado pearls and creamy coconut milk. You can also add fresh fruits—such as durian, coconut and avocado—for an even better flavor. Trust me, the combination will never disappoint.

Avocado Pudding

½ cup (120 ml) cold water

2¼ tbsp (20 g) powdered gelatin

1½ lb (680 g) avocado

½ cup (120 ml) coconut milk

½ cup (120 ml) milk

⅓ cup (80 ml) sweetened condensed milk

⅓ cup (67 g) sugar

Avocado Pearls

⅔ cup (80 g) tapioca starch, plus more if needed

2 tbsp (26 g) sugar, divided

2 oz (60 g) avocado

1 tbsp (15 ml) boiling water

To make the avocado pudding, first prepare the pudding molds. This recipe requires six molds, such as Pyrex cups or ceramic ramekins, each with a volume of 210 milliliters (a little under 1 cup).

Pour the cold water into a small bowl, sprinkle in the powdered gelatin and stir well. Allow the gelatin to bloom for 5 minutes. Melt the gelatin in a microwave for 10 to 15 seconds on medium or by placing the bowl in a larger bowl of hot water and stirring.

In a blender, blend the avocado, coconut milk, milk, condensed milk and sugar until smooth. Pour the mixture into a large bowl and whisk in the melted gelatin.

Divide the mixture equally among six pudding molds. To keep the pudding from turning brown from oxidation, cover the molds with plastic wrap. Refrigerate the puddings for at least 6 hours before serving. This avocado pudding can be stored in the refrigerator for up to 3 days.

To make avocado pearls, in a small bowl, combine the tapioca starch and 1 tablespoon (13 g) of the sugar. Add the avocado, crush it with your hands and mix it into the tapioca starch. Pour in the boiling water and knead the dough until it is smooth and elastic. If your dough is still sticky, add some tapioca starch. If it's still dry, some hot water should do the trick. Form the dough into ⅓-inch (1-cm) pearls.

Bring a medium-sized saucepan of water to a boil over medium-high heat, then drop in the pearls. Cook them for about 3 minutes, or until they float to the surface. After that, transfer to a bowl of cold water to cool. Once cooled, drain the water and mix the pearls with the remaining tablespoon (13 g) of sugar. Let the sugared pearls rest for 30 minutes before serving.

(continued)

Avocado Pudding with Coconut Milk Sauce (Continued)

Blue Jelly

1 tsp agar-agar powder

1¼ cups (300 ml) coconut water or water

10 butterfly pea flowers, or blue food coloring

2 tbsp (26 g) sugar

Toppings

Shaved ice

Cubed avocado

Young coconut meat

Durian flesh (seedless)

Coconut Milk Sauce (page 14), for serving

Toasted coconut flakes

To make the blue jelly, in a small saucepan off the heat, combine the agar-agar powder and coconut water and soak for around 30 minutes. Over medium heat, stir the mixture until it comes to a boil. Add the butterfly pea flowers and boil for another 5 minutes, then remove and discard them. Lower the heat to medium-low, whisk in the sugar and simmer for another 1 to 2 minutes before removing from the heat. Pour the jelly into a 6-inch (15-cm) square cake pan and place in the refrigerator to chill fully. Before serving, cut the jelly into small cubes or long strips as desired.

Soak the chilled pudding molds in hot water for 5 seconds and flip over onto a dessert dish to remove the pudding from the molds. To assemble the dessert, start by filling an individual dessert bowl halfway with shaved ice. Place an avocado pudding in the middle, then arrange one-sixth of the jellies, pearls, avocado, young coconut meat and durian on top of the ice. Drizzle Coconut Milk Sauce on top and sprinkle with toasted coconut flakes.

Sweet Potato Balls Dessert (Che Khoai Deo)

Yield:
6 servings

In recent years, the Taiwanese dessert of taro and sweet potato balls has become very popular among foodies in Vietnam. This colorful dish is made up of sweet potato and taro balls, often paired with red beans and grass jelly. While the original version is served with ginger syrup, Vietnamese people prefer to enjoy this dessert with a creamy coconut milk mixture. It's the perfect treat to cool down with on hot days and should definitely be on your list of must-try desserts.

Rolled Balls

4 oz (115 g) sweet potato, peeled and cubed

4 oz (115 g) purple sweet potato, peeled and cubed

4 oz (115 g) taro, peeled and cubed

3 tsp (13 g) granulated sugar

1½ cups (180 g) tapioca starch, plus more if needed

Grass Jelly

1 oz (30 g) grass jelly powder

2 tbsp (26 g) granulated sugar

2¼ cups (535 ml) water, divided

To make the rolled balls, prepare a steamer with water and bring to a boil over medium-high heat. Steam the sweet potato, purple potato and taro together for about 20 minutes, or until soft. Once they're cooked, transfer by kind into three separate medium-sized bowls, add a teaspoon of granulated sugar to each and mash with a fork while still hot. Then, add ½ cup (60 g) of the tapioca starch to each bowl and knead until you have three dough balls that are smooth and free from any dry flour. If the dough is sticky, add a little more tapioca starch; if it's dry, add a small amount of boiling water.

Divide each dough ball in half and roll each portion into a long rope about ⅜ inch (1 cm) in diameter. Cut the ropes into segments about 1¼ inches (3 cm) in length and form into small balls. In a large saucepan, bring water to a boil over medium-high heat, drop in the balls and cook for 5 to 7 minutes, or until they float to the top. Remove the balls from the water and transfer them to a bowl of iced water. Let them soak until completely cooled, then drain the water.

To make the grass jelly, in a small bowl, combine the grass jelly powder and granulated sugar with 1¼ cups (300 ml) of the water until fully incorporated. Then, add the remaining cup (240 ml) of water and stir well. Let sit for about 10 minutes. Next, strain the mixture through a fine-mesh sieve into a small saucepan and place over medium heat. Stir the mixture for 3 to 5 minutes, or until smooth, and then turn off the heat. Carefully pour the mixture into a heatproof 6-inch (15-cm) square glass cake pan and let it cool to room temperature. Once cool, the jelly will become firm. Keep it in the fridge until you're ready to serve.

(continued)

Sweet Potato Balls Dessert (Continued)

Taro Paste

8 oz (225 g) taro

⅓ cup (80 ml) sweetened condensed milk

2 tbsp (28 g) unsalted butter, melted

Sweet Red Beans

4 oz (115 g) dried red beans, soaked in water overnight, then drained, or 12 oz (340 g) canned, drained

2 cups (475 ml) water

½ tsp salt

3 tbsp (39 g) granulated sugar

Creamy Coconut Milk

1⅔ cups (400 ml) canned coconut milk

¾ cup (180 ml) milk

5 oz (140 g) rock sugar

Shaved ice, for serving

To make the taro paste, in a steamer, steam the taro for 20 minutes, or until soft. If desired, you can steam it in the same steamer with the other vegetables in the first step, to save time. In a small bowl, mash the cooked taro with the condensed milk and butter until you achieve a rough texture. Then, transfer the mixture to a medium-sized nonstick skillet and cook over medium heat, stirring frequently with a spatula. Cook until the steam evaporates and the mixture forms a dry paste, which usually takes 2 to 3 minutes. Remove from the heat, cover the paste with plastic wrap and let it cool before serving.

To make sweet red beans, if using dried beans, in a medium-sized saucepan, combine the drained red beans with the water and salt. Bring to a boil over high heat, then lower the heat to medium-low and simmer for 1½ to 2 hours, or until the beans are soft and tender. Drain the beans and return them to the saucepan along with the granulated sugar. Stir the mixture continuously over medium-low heat for 7 to 10 minutes to help the sugar dissolve and soak into the beans. Then, remove from the heat and let cool to room temperature. For canned red beans, rinse them with water and follow the same process of stirring in the sugar.

To make the creamy coconut milk, in a medium-sized saucepan, combine the coconut milk, milk and rock sugar. Heat over medium-low heat, stirring constantly, until the sugar has dissolved and the mixture comes to a boil. Remove from the heat and let cool to room temperature. Once cooled, transfer the sauce to a container with a lid and refrigerate until ready to use.

To serve, fill a large bowl half full with shaved ice. Next, add the taro balls, sweet potato balls, purple sweet potato balls, grass jelly, taro paste and sweet red beans. Finish by drizzling the creamy coconut milk over the top of the dessert.

Mango Noodle Jelly in Coconut Milk Sauce
(Che Hu Tieu Xoai)

When you first hear the title of this dessert, you might find it strange to have noodles in a sweet dish. But don't worry! The noodles here refer to a type of coconut milk jelly that looks like a flat noodle called *hu tieu det* in Vietnam. This unique dessert is a spin-off from mango sago, a dessert of Hong Kong origin. You can prepare the ingredients in advance, store them in the refrigerator for 3 to 4 days and combine them whenever you want to eat. Trust me, this special mango dessert is sure to amaze and delight your taste buds.

Mango Pudding

½ cup (120 ml) cold water

2¼ tbsp (20 g) powdered gelatin

1¼ cups (300 ml) milk

1¼ cups (300 ml) heavy cream

½ cup (100 g) granulated sugar

1 lb (455 g) mango

Flat Noodle Jelly

1 tbsp (9 g) konnyaku jelly powder (see page 150)

½ cup (100 g) granulated sugar

1¼ cups (300 ml) water

2 cups (460 g) yogurt

1¼ cups (300 ml) milk

To make the mango pudding, gather six molds, such as Pyrex cups or ceramic ramekins, each with a volume of 210 milliliters (a little under 1 cup).

Pour the cold water into a small bowl, sprinkle in the powdered gelatin and stir well. Allow the gelatin to bloom for 5 minutes. In a small saucepan, combine the milk, cream and granulated sugar. Stir the mixture over medium-low heat to dissolve the sugar. Remove from the heat when it starts to steam. Add the bloomed gelatin and stir well. Puree the mango until smooth, then pour it into the milk mixture and stir until incorporated.

Divide the mixture equally among the six molds. To keep the pudding from turning brown from oxidation, cover the molds with plastic wrap. Refrigerate for at least 6 hours before serving. This mango pudding can be stored in the fridge for up to 3 days.

To make flat noodle jelly, in a small bowl, mix together the konnyaku jelly powder and granulated sugar. In a medium-sized saucepan, bring the water to a boil. Gradually add the jelly powder mixture to the water while stirring to prevent clumping. Continue to heat the mixture for 2 minutes, then remove it from the heat. Add the yogurt and milk and stir well to incorporate.

Pour the jelly mixture into a 9 x 13–inch (23 x 33–cm) rectangular cake pan or in a container of your choice, then allow it to cool completely at room temperature. Once fully set, chill in the fridge until ready to serve. Before serving, slice the jelly into thin, long strands about ½ inch (1.3 cm) wide resembling the look of Vietnamese flat noodles.

(continued)

Mango Noodle Jelly in Coconut Milk Sauce (Continued)

Tapioca Noodles

½ cup (120 ml) water

¾ cup (165 g) dark brown sugar, divided

⅔ cup (80 g) + 2 tbsp (15 g) tapioca starch, divided, plus more if needed

2 tbsp (10 g) unsweetened cocoa powder

Sago

6 oz (170 g) sago

6 cups (1.4 L) water, divided

Mango Puree

1 lb (455 g) mango flesh

⅔ cup (160 ml) milk

¼ cup (60 ml) sweetened condensed milk

Shaved ice, for serving

Cubed mangoes, for serving

Creamy Coconut Milk (page 102)

To make the tapioca noodles, in a small saucepan, combine the water, ½ cup (110 g) of the brown sugar and 1 tablespoon (8 g) of tapioca starch from the ⅔ cup (80 g) you measured of it. Stir the mixture over medium heat until it thickens to a sticky translucent consistency, then turn off the heat. Add the remaining tapioca starch (72 g) from the ⅔ cup (80 g) plus the cocoa powder, and mix until well combined. Knead with your hands until you have a smooth, nonsticky dough. If your dough is still sticky, add some tapioca starch. If it's still dry, some hot water should do the trick.

Using a rolling pin, flatten the dough to a thickness of ¼ inch (6 mm), then cut it into small fibers about 1½ inches (4 cm) long. Dust the remaining 2 tablespoons (15 g) of the tapioca starch all over the noodles to keep them from sticking together. The purpose of this step is to create long noodles to enhance the visual appeal of the dessert, but you can also roll the dough into small balls and make regular pearls.

Bring a medium-sized saucepan of water to a boil over medium-high heat, then add the noodles. Cook for about 20 minutes, or until they float to the surface. Once the noodles have floated, turn off the heat, cover the pot and let them incubate for 20 minutes to thoroughly cook them. Then, transfer to a bowl of cold water to cool. Once cooled, drain the noodles and mix with the remaining ¼ cup (55 g) of brown sugar. Let sit for at least 15 minutes before using.

To make the sago, soak it in 2 cups (475 ml) of water for 20 minutes, then drain. Next, in a medium-sized saucepan, bring 4 cups (946 ml) of water to a boil and add the drained sago. Let the sago simmer for 15 minutes, then remove from the heat, rinse with cold water and drain well.

Last but not least, to make the mango puree, in a blender, blend the mango with the milk and condensed milk until smooth.

Soak the mango pudding molds in hot water for 5 seconds, then flip over onto a plate to remove the puddings from the molds. To assemble the dessert, fill an individual dessert bowl halfway with shaved ice. Place a mango pudding in the middle, then arrange one-sixth of the jellies, noodles, sago, mango puree and cubed mangoes on top of the ice. Drizzle creamy coconut milk over it all and enjoy.

Breads and Bao Buns

This chapter delves into the delicious world of bread and bao buns, two favorite and beloved dishes of Vietnamese people.

First, we will dive into the world of Vietnamese bread and explore its most popular dishes. The star of the show is undoubtedly the banh mi, a unique bread with a crispy exterior and a soft, fluffy interior that serves as the perfect base for a variety of fillings. In the opening recipe of this chapter (page 109), I will guide you through the process of making banh mi from scratch, allowing you to customize it with your pre-ferred meats and salad ingredients. We will also take a closer look at the Vietnamese-style brioche bread (page 111), which has its own distinct characteristics that set it apart from the original recipe. Additionally, we will discover other beloved bread recipes in Vietnam, including a savory cheese-filled bread (page 121), a tropical coconut milk bun (page 115) and a coffee-coated bread (page 117) inspired by our Malaysian friends. These dishes offer a multicultural and flavorful culinary experience that you can savor and enjoy in Vietnam.

Nearly half of the remaining content of this chapter will revolve around the sweet bao buns that have won the hearts of many Vietnamese people. These buns were first introduced to Vietnam through the influence of Chinese culinary culture and have since become a beloved staple in our cuisine. Among the different varieties of sweet bao buns, liu sha bao (page 127), with its irresistible molten lava salted egg filling, has become a favorite among locals. Additionally, you'll discover how to make bao buns with a golden custard filling (page 123), and the unique durian pulp bao buns (page 129) that boast a fully tropical flavor.

Vietnamese Baguettes (Banh Mi Viet Nam)

Banh mi, a Vietnamese dish originating from French cuisine, has been adapted by Vietnamese cuisine to suit local tastes. The bread loaf is typically around 7 inches (18 cm) long, with a crispy outer shell and a soft, spongy interior. It is a well-known dish among international friends and is often filled with such ingredients as meat, pâté and vegetables. Vietnamese people enjoy banh mi at any time of the day, either as a meal replacement or to satisfy their hunger.

Poolish

½ cup (70 g) bread flour, sifted

1 tsp instant yeast

¼ cup (60 ml) water

Main Dough

½ cup (120 ml) cold water

1 large egg, cold

1½ tsp (7 g) sugar

1 tsp instant yeast

2 cups (275 g) bread flour, sifted, plus more for dusting, if needed

¼ tsp salt

1 tsp neutral oil or melted unsalted butter, plus more for shaping and bowl

To make the poolish, in a medium-sized bowl (big enough for the poolish to grow two to three times its original size), mix together the bread flour, instant yeast and water. Cover the bowl with plastic wrap and let the dough ferment at room temperature for 6 to 8 hours or overnight. If you haven't used the poolish immediately after fermentation, store it in the refrigerator for up to 3 days.

To make the main dough, in the bowl of a stand mixer, use a wooden spoon to mix together the cold water and egg. Then, using the whisk attachment, whisk in the sugar and instant yeast. Add the sifted bread flour, poolish and salt to the bowl, change to a dough hook attachment and knead at a slow speed until the ingredients are well combined and no dry flour remains.

Next, add the oil and continue to knead at medium speed for another 15 minutes. Finally, increase the speed to high and knead for 5 minutes before stopping. You will know the dough is ready when it has a smooth, shiny surface and can be stretched into a thin film that allows light to pass through.

Coat your palms with a little bit of oil and shape the dough into a smooth round ball. Apply a thin layer of oil or butter to the bowl, place the dough inside and cover with plastic wrap. Place the bowl on the middle rack of an unheated oven, and set a cup of hot water on the bottom of the oven. Let the dough rise for about an hour, or until it has doubled in size.

After fermentation, divide the dough into six equal-sized portions of about 3.5 ounces (100 g) each. Roll each portion into a smooth round ball. Cover the balls with a damp, clean towel to prevent drying.

(continued)

Vietnamese Baguettes (Continued)

Working with one ball of dough at a time, use a rolling pin to flatten the dough into a 3 x 9-inch (7.5 x 23–cm) rectangle. On one 3-inch (7.5-cm) edge, fold the two dough edges diagonally toward the middle (the fold line should be about 5½ inches [14 cm] long). Roll the dough tightly from the outside using your hands, and pinch the seam securely. Make a 30-degree angle with your palms and roll the ends of the dough to create a smaller pointed tip compared to the middle.

Place the shaped doughs on a baguette baking pan, leaving about 2 inches (5 cm) of room for it to rise and expand. Cover the shaped dough with a piece of cheesecloth to prevent drying. Repeat the process with the remaining dough. Note: If you don't have a baguette pan, you can use a cotton pastry cloth. Sprinkle a light layer of flour on the cloth and make grooves about 3 inches (7.5 cm) apart to fit the formed baguettes and prevent them from sticking together after proofing. When transferring the formed baguettes to the prepared pan, be gentle so as to keep their shape as much as possible. Alternatively, use a normal pan and alternate the stacking of the formed baguettes to allow space for them to expand.

Put the pan on the middle rack of an unheated oven, and put a cup of hot water on the bottom of the oven. Allow the doughs to rise for 30 to 45 minutes, or until they have doubled in size. You can check by gently pressing your finger on the surface of the dough and watching it gently inflate. Remove the pan from the oven and let it sit at room temperature for another 15 minutes. Meanwhile, heat the oven to 450°F (230°C) with the oven fan turned off.

Spray a thin layer of water onto the surface of each baguette dough and make a shallow cut about ¼ inch (6 mm) deep along the top using a clean razor blade or sharp knife. Before placing the pan in the oven, spray a light layer of water into the cut.

Fill a baking pan with boiling water and place it on the bottom rack of the oven to produce steam during baking. Place the baguette pan on the middle rack and bake for 20 minutes. After 15 minutes, you can rotate the baguette pan to evenly brown the loaves on all sides.

Once the breads are finished baking, remove from the oven and let cool completely. About 5 minutes after baking, you should hear the crust cracking, which indicates that you have successfully made a batch of banh mi.

Banh mi has a thin, crunchy crust and the inside is soft and very light. If you don't eat it all, put the leftovers in a ziplock bag. Reheat the bread in the oven for a few minutes before eating to make it crisp again.

Vietnamese Brioche Breads (Banh Mi Hoa Cuc)

Yield: 2 brioche loaves

Originating from France, brioche is one of the most loved sweet breads in Vietnam, and this is a Vietnamese modification of this classic bread. Vietnamese people have refined and adapted brioche to fit local culture and taste, given the differences in climate and ingredients. The name *hoa cuc* (chrysanthemum) comes from the texture of the bread, with many yellow "fibers" stacked like chrysanthemum petals. There are many shapes that can be created with traditional brioche, but Vietnamese bakers typically braid the bread to create a distinctive identity for this bread. This is a great choice for breakfast when paired with hot milk.

¼ cup (60 ml) milk, cold

3 tbsp (45 ml) heavy cream, cold

3 tbsp (15 g) milk powder

1 large egg, cold

2 tsp (10 ml) orange blossom water or vanilla extract

¼ cup (50 g) sugar

1½ tsp (4.5 g) instant yeast

2 cups (275 g) bread flour, sifted, plus more for dusting

¼ tsp salt

½ cup (1 stick, 114 g) cold unsalted butter, sliced thinly (see Note)

Neutral oil, for shaping and bowl

Melted unsalted butter, for pan

1 tbsp (15 ml) milk, at room temperature

1 tsp honey

Sliced almonds, for garnish

In the bowl of a stand mixer, combine the cold milk, cream, milk powder, egg and orange blossom water, and mix well with a wooden spoon. Then, add the whisk attachment and whisk in the sugar and instant yeast. Add the sifted bread flour and salt, change to the dough hook attachment and knead at a slow speed until the ingredients are well combined and no dry flour remains.

Increase the speed to medium and knead for an additional 10 minutes. Add the sliced butter gradually and continue to knead for another 10 minutes, or until the butter is fully mixed in and the dough is smooth, shiny and elastic. The dough should pass the windowpane test, meaning it can be stretched into a thin film that allows light to pass through.

Lightly oil your palms and remove the dough from the bowl. Form the dough into a round shape, then evenly coat it with oil. Place the dough in a large ziplock bag and store in the fridge for 6 to 8 hours or overnight. This slow fermentation process will enhance the taste and texture of the final product.

After fermentation, remove the dough from the fridge and press it to deflate the air inside. Divide the dough into six equal-sized portions. Use a rolling pin to roll a portion into a 3 x 4-inch (7.5 x 10-cm) rectangle. Use your hands to roll the dough lengthwise from the outside in to form a long roll. Wrap each roll with plastic wrap and put in the fridge while shaping the remaining pieces of dough.

Prepare two oval baking pans, each about 9 inches (23 cm) long, 2½ inches (6.5 cm) across and 4½ inches (11.5 cm) deep. Butter the pans with melted butter and dust with flour.

(continued)

Vietnamese Brioche Breads (Continued)

Remove one dough roll from the fridge and roll it into a long rope about 13 inches (33 cm) long, or one and a half times the length of the pans. Repeat with the remaining two pieces of dough, then braid all three together and place in one prepared pan. Repeat with the remaining three dough rolls, placing the braided dough in the second prepared pan. Cover each pan with a damp, clean cloth and let rise in a warm place for 1½ to 2 hours, or until the dough fills two-thirds of each pan.

Next, preheat the oven to 350°F (180°C). In a small bowl, mix together the milk and honey and brush it over the surface of the dough. Then, sprinkle sliced almonds on the top.

Place the two bread pans on the second rack from the bottom of the oven, and place a small skillet filled with boiling water in the middle of the bottom rack to maintain moisture during baking. Bake for 20 to 25 minutes. Once the bread is done baking, remove from the oven and brush the surface with melted butter, giving it a shiny and appetizing appearance (if desired).

Brioche bread should be eaten fresh for the best taste and texture. Enjoy the rich and soft texture of brioche bread for breakfast, as a snack or as the base for your favorite sandwich. If you need to store it, place your bread in a ziplock bag or sealed container and keep at room temperature for up to 4 days, or in the fridge for up to 10 days.

Note: The recipe calls for a large amount of butter, which may take longer to fully incorporate into the dough during kneading. This long process can cause the temperature to rise, which can cause the butter to melt. If this happens, stop kneading and put the dough in the freezer for 5 minutes. Then, resume kneading as normal.

Coconut Milk Buns (Banh Mi Sua Dua)

Yield: 8 buns

Coconut is an indispensable ingredient in Vietnamese cakes and desserts, and it is no exception when it comes to bread. The coconut milk bun is a soft and fluffy bread filled with a sweet and fragrant coconut custard filling. Every bite of this bread will transport you to Southeast Asia with its delicious flavor. It is the perfect treat to enjoy on chilly days, especially when paired with a cup of tea, coffee or hot milk.

Coconut Filling

1 large egg

2 tbsp (36 g) sugar

2 tbsp (28 g) unsalted butter, melted

2 tbsp (30 ml) canned coconut milk

1 tbsp (15 ml) sweetened condensed milk

¾ cup (70 g) desiccated coconut

Milk Dough

½ cup + 2 tbsp (150 ml) milk

1 large egg

1 tbsp (13 g) sugar

1½ tsp (4.5 g) instant yeast

2 cups (275 g) bread flour, sifted

¼ tsp salt

2 tbsp (28 g) unsalted butter, at room temperature

Neutral oil or melted butter, for bowl

To make the coconut filling, in a small bowl, mix together the egg and sugar until smooth. Then, add the melted butter, coconut milk and condensed milk, stirring until everything is incorporated. Finally, mix in the desiccated coconut until well combined. Cover the bowl with plastic wrap and put in the fridge until ready to use.

To make the milk dough, in a large bowl, combine the milk and egg. Next, whisk in the sugar and instant yeast. Add the sifted bread flour and salt, and use a wooden spoon or spatula to mix everything together until no dry flour remains.

Transfer the dough to a clean work surface and knead by hand for 10 minutes, or until smooth. Add the butter and keep kneading for another 10 minutes, or until the butter is fully mixed in and the dough is smooth, shiny and elastic. If you have a stand mixer, you can use it to knead the dough more easily.

Form the dough into a smooth round ball. Oil or butter a bowl and put the dough inside. Wrap the bowl with plastic wrap and let the dough rise in a warm place for 45 to 60 minutes, or until doubled in size.

After fermentation, press the dough to deflate the air inside. Then, divide it into eight equal-sized portions of around ¼ cup (60 g) each. Roll each portion into a smooth round ball. Cover the balls with a damp, clean towel to prevent drying. Working with one ball at a time, use a rolling pin to flatten the dough into a 5 x 10–inch (13 x 25-cm) rectangle.

Divide the coconut filling into eight equal-sized portions. Take one portion and spread it evenly on a dough rectangle, leaving a bare margin of about ½ inch (1.3 cm) around the edges. Roll the dough lengthwise and secure the seam by pinching it firmly. Cut the roll in half lengthwise, leaving the top end connected. Twist the two sections together, roll up the twisted dough and press the ends together. Place the roll on a baking sheet lined with parchment paper, leaving 2 inches (5 cm) of room between the rolls. Repeat the process with the remaining dough.

(continued)

Coconut Milk Buns (Continued)

Egg Wash

1 large egg yolk

2 tsp (10 ml) milk

Sliced almonds, for garnish

Cover the rolls with plastic wrap and let rise in a warm place for 30 to 45 minutes, or until they have doubled in size. Meanwhile, preheat the oven to 350°F (180°C).

Before baking, in a small bowl, stir together the egg yolk and milk, lightly brush the rolls with the egg wash mixture and sprinkle sliced almonds on top. Place the baking sheet on the second rack from the bottom of the oven and bake for 20 minutes, or until the buns are golden brown all over.

To fully enjoy the delicious taste of coconut milk buns, you should eat them while they are still warm and fresh, within a day. To store the buns, place them in a ziplock bag or sealed container and keep them at room temperature for up to 4 days, or in the fridge for up to 10 days.

Coffee Buns (Banh Mi Pappa Roti)

This bread, which originated in Malaysia, has gained immense popularity among Vietnamese people since its introduction in Vietnam. Besides the name *pappa roti*, it is also known by several other names, such as coffee buns, Mexican buns and roti boys. The bread's unique feature is the aromatic coffee scent emitted by its crispy coffee topping, which envelops the tender and fluffy bread inside. While these coffee buns are already delightful on their own, pairing them with a hot cup of coffee or milk makes for a perfect breakfast that one cannot resist.

Yield:
6 buns

Sweet Dough

⅓ cup + 1 tbsp (95 ml) milk

1 large egg

3 tbsp (39 g) sugar

1 tsp instant yeast

1½ cups (205 g) bread flour, sifted

⅓ tsp salt

2 tbsp (28 g) unsalted butter, at room temperature

Neutral oil or melted butter, for bowl

2 tbsp (28 g) salted butter, cold, cut into 6 cubes

To make the sweet dough, in a large bowl, mix together the milk and egg. Then, whisk in the sugar and instant yeast. Add the sifted bread flour and salt, and use a wooden spoon or spatula to mix everything together until no dry flour remains.

Transfer the dough to a clean work surface and knead by hand for 10 minutes, or until smooth. Then, add the unsalted butter and continue to knead for another 10 minutes, or until the butter is fully mixed in and the dough is smooth, shiny and elastic. If you have a stand mixer, you can use it to knead the dough more easily.

Form the dough into a smooth round ball. Oil a bowl with oil or melted butter and put the dough inside. Wrap the bowl with plastic wrap and let rise in a warm place for 45 to 60 minutes, or until doubled in size.

After fermentation, press the dough to deflate the air inside. Then divide into six equal-sized portions of around ¼ cup (60 g) each. Roll each portion into a smooth round ball. Cover the balls with a damp, clean towel to prevent drying.

Working with one ball at a time, flatten a ball of dough using your palms. Place a cube of cold salted butter in the center and wrap the opposite sides of the dough together, making sure to tightly seal the seam to prevent the butter from leaking out during baking. Place the assembled bun on a baking sheet lined with parchment paper. Repeat the process with the remaining dough, leaving 2 inches (5 cm) of room between the buns. Cover the assembled buns with plastic wrap and let rise in a warm place for 20 to 30 minutes, or until they have doubled in size.

(continued)

Coffee Buns (Continued)

Coffee Topping

1 tbsp (6 g) instant coffee powder

1 tbsp (15 ml) boiling water

4 tbsp (½ stick, 55 g) unsalted butter, at room temperature

2 tbsp (26 g) sugar

1 large egg yolk

½ cup (60 g) cake flour

½ tsp unsweetened cocoa powder

Dark and white chocolate buttons (optional)

To make the coffee topping, in a glass liquid measuring cup, combine the coffee powder with the boiling water. In a separate bowl, mix together the butter and sugar, then whisk in the egg yolk and the coffee mixture. Sift in the cake flour and cocoa powder, and stir until the mixture is smooth and no dry flour remains. Transfer this coffee topping to a piping bag.

Meanwhile, preheat the oven to 350°F (180°C). Pipe the topping onto the buns in spirals until they are about two-thirds covered. Place the pan on the second rack from the bottom of the oven and bake for 20 to 25 minutes.

Remove from the oven and transfer the buns to a wire rack. Wait 5 minutes for the buns to cool down and the coffee crust to get crispier. Store any leftover buns in an airtight bag or container for up to 3 days at room temperature, or 5 days in the fridge. Reheat the buns by baking at 350°F (180°C) for 5 minutes.

To transform your coffee buns into adorable bear buns, start by preparing melted chocolate per the instructions on page 80. Let your creativity take over and have fun designing your very own cute bear buns. I would be delighted if my bear bun recipe inspires friends from around the world to create their own adorable versions.

Meat Floss Lava Cheese Loaves
(Banh Mi Pho Mai Cha Bong)

Vietnamese people have a particular fondness for cakes or bread that have a creamy and flowing filling. This is why we are particularly drawn to a sweet and savory bread that is adorned with meat floss and has a cheese custard filling that runs out when bitten into. This bread is always a top seller at local bakeries and is very popular among Vietnamese people. You can prepare the ingredients separately and assemble the bread whenever you want to eat, making it a simple and convenient option.

Yield:
4 loaves

Bread Dough

½ cup + 2 tbsp (150 ml) milk, plus more for brushing

1 large egg

2 tbsp (26 g) sugar

1 tsp instant yeast

2 cups (275 g) bread flour, sifted, plus more for dusting

⅓ tsp salt

2 tbsp (28 g) unsalted butter, at room temperature

Neutral oil or melted butter, for bowl

Melted unsalted butter, for pans

To make the bread dough, in a large bowl, combine the milk and egg. Then, whisk in the sugar and instant yeast. Add the sifted bread flour and salt to the bowl, then use a wooden spoon or spatula to mix everything together until no dry flour remains.

Transfer the dough to a clean work surface and knead by hand for 10 minutes, or until smooth. Add the butter and keep kneading for another 10 minutes, or until the butter is fully mixed in and the dough is smooth, shiny and elastic. If you have a stand mixer, you can use it to knead the dough more easily.

Form the dough into a smooth round ball. Oil a bowl with oil or melted butter and put the dough inside. Wrap the bowl with plastic wrap and let the dough rise in a warm place for 45 to 60 minutes, or until doubled in size.

After fermentation, press the dough to deflate the air inside. Then, weigh and divide the dough into four equal-sized portions. Roll each portion into a smooth round ball. Cover the balls with a damp, clean towel to prevent drying.

Select four loaf pans measuring 6 x 3 inches (15 x 7.5 cm). Butter the pans with melted butter and dust with bread flour. If you do not have loaf pans, just divide and shape the dough into round or elongated balls to the size you desire and place on a baking sheet lined with parchment paper, leaving 2 inches (5 cm) of room between the buns.

(continued)

Meat Floss Lava Cheese Loaves (Continued)

Cream Cheese Filling

5 oz (140 g) cream cheese, at room temperature

⅓ cup (67 g) sugar

⅓ tsp salt

1 tbsp (8 g) cornstarch

¾ cup (180 ml) milk

½ cup (120 ml) heavy cream

2 tbsp (28 g) unsalted butter

Pork or chicken floss (see page 151), for topping

Use a rolling pin to roll one dough ball into a rectangle whose short side measures the same as the long side of your loaf pan. Roll it tightly into a loaf along the short side and pinch the edges to seal, then place in a prepared pan. Repeat with the remaining dough and remaining pan. Cover the loaves with plastic wrap or a clean towel and let rise in a warm place for 30 to 45 minutes, or until they have doubled in size.

Meanwhile, preheat the oven to 350°F (180°C). Before baking, lightly brush milk on the loaves' surface. Place the pans on the second rack from the bottom of the oven and bake for 20 to 25 minutes. Once done, take the loaves out, unmold them and put them on the rack to cool down.

To make the cream cheese filling, in a medium-sized bowl, combine the softened cream cheese, sugar and salt and blend together well. Next, add the cornstarch, milk and cream, and whisk until fully incorporated. Strain the mixture through a mesh sieve into a medium-sized saucepan to remove any lumps. Place over medium-low heat and stir constantly for about 3 minutes, until the filling gets a little thicker but still flows like a paste. Turn off the heat, add the butter and mix well. Cover the filling with plastic wrap and let cool completely before transferring it to a piping bag or squeeze bottle.

Poke two holes in the top of a loaf with a chopstick, deep enough to hold a decent amount of filling. Fill the holes with the cream cheese filling and spread a layer over the top of the loaf. Add your desired amount of meat floss on top, gently pressing it onto the bread to help it stick. Repeat with the remaining loaves.

For best flavor, eat the loaves within 4 hours after adding the filling and meat floss. If you're not ready to serve, store each component separately in the fridge and enjoy within 3 days.

Custard Bao Buns (Banh Bao Cadé)

Yield: 10 or
11 buns

This bun is a popular Vietnamese delicacy filled with a delightful yellow custard that can be enjoyed at any time of day. The term *cadé* comes from the Malay word *kaya*, which means "rich" and refers to a type of jam made from coconut milk, eggs and caramel sugar. The original Malaysian kaya sauce has a brown color similar to peanut butter, but in Vietnam, the recipe has evolved to produce a shiny yellow sauce using sugar or condensed milk for sweetness instead of caramel. In addition to being used as a filling for bao buns, this sauce is also used by Vietnamese people as a topping for sticky rice or as a filling for bread.

Custard Filling

1 tbsp (10 g) custard powder

1½ tbsp (12 g) cornstarch or cake flour

1 tbsp (13 g) sugar

1 large egg

2 tbsp (30 ml) milk

2 tbsp (30 ml) canned coconut milk

2 tbsp (30 ml) sweetened condensed milk

2 tbsp (28 g) unsalted butter

Bao Dough

½ cup (120 ml) milk, cold

¾ tsp instant yeast

1½ tbsp (20 g) sugar

1⅓ cups (165 g) all-purpose flour, sifted

¼ cup (30 g) cake flour, sifted

1½ tsp (7 ml) neutral oil or melted unsalted butter

To make the custard filling, in a small bowl, whisk together the custard powder, cornstarch and sugar. Then, add the egg, milk, coconut milk and condensed milk in the middle and stir until well combined. Strain the mixture through a fine-mesh sieve into a small saucepan.

Stir the mixture over medium-low heat for 8 to 10 minutes, or until it thickens, becomes smooth and pliable and no longer sticks to the pan. Once thick, turn off the heat and stir in the butter until fully melted and absorbed into the custard. Transfer the custard to a heatproof container, cover with plastic wrap and allow it to cool completely before refrigerating for an hour.

Divide the filling into ten or eleven equal-sized portions, each being about 1 level tablespoon (15 g). Place on a plate or baking sheet, cover with plastic wrap and keep in the fridge until needed.

To make the dough, in a small bowl, combine the milk, yeast, sugar, all-purpose flour, cake flour and oil, and mix well with a wooden spoon or spatula until no dry flour remains. Transfer the dough to a clean work surface and knead for 10 to 12 minutes, or until smooth and elastic.

Divide the dough into ten or eleven equal-sized portions, about 2 level tablespoons (30 g) each. Cover with plastic wrap or a damp, clean towel to prevent drying out.

Working with five dough portions at a time, knead each for 2 to 3 minutes, or until soft and pliable with a smooth texture. Use your palms to tuck and press until a ball is formed. Place the ball smooth side down and roll it out into a 3-inch (7.5-cm)-diameter circle with thin edges and a thick center. Repeat with the remaining dough.

(continued)

Custard Bao Buns (Continued)

Place the filling in the middle of the dough, wrap the edges around the filling to cover it and make sure the seam is tightly sealed to prevent leaks while steaming. Then, use your palms to rotate and elongate the dough ball as high as possible to prevent it from flattening when steamed. Place each bun inside a paper liner that has been placed in a mini tart mold. Repeat the process with the remaining dough and filling.

Fill the steamer pot with water to a 1½-inch (4-cm) depth. Heat the water to a temperature of 110°F (45°C) and then turn off the heat. Place the buns in the steamer basket and place the basket on top of the pot. Partially cover with the lid, opened by about ½ inch (1.3 cm). Let the buns proof for 60 minutes, or until they have increased in size by 60 percent. You can test whether they are ready by gently pressing the surface of a bun and observing if it slowly rises again.

Remove the steamer basket from the pot and bring the water in the pot to a boil over high heat. Then, lower the heat to medium. To prevent water droplets from falling on the buns during steaming, wrap the steamer lid with a clean cloth. Place the basket of proofed buns over the pot, cover fully and steam for 8 minutes.

Once the steaming is done, turn off the heat and let the bao buns sit in the steamer basket for 5 minutes to keep them from collapsing. Then, open the lid and take them out of the steamer to serve.

For the best experience, it's recommended to consume the custard buns when they are warm. The leftover custard buns can be stored in a sealed container or plastic bag in the fridge for up to 2 days, or in the freezer for about a month. To reheat the buns, simply steam them for 5 minutes.

Salted Egg Yolk Lava Bao Buns
(Banh Bao Kim Sa)

Yield: 10 or 11 buns

These are a beloved sweet treat in Vietnamese cuisine. While originally from Chinese cuisine, the buns have been adapted to suit Vietnamese tastes. With a soft, spongy dough and a sweet and salty egg filling, they offer an irresistible flavor. The dough can come in different colors, such as white, yellow or black from bamboo charcoal. Salted egg yolk lava bao buns can be enjoyed any time of day, whether as a breakfast or a light snack.

Salted Egg Filling

4 salted egg yolks (see page 150)

1 tbsp (10 g) custard powder

1 tbsp (5 g) milk powder

1 tbsp (8 g) cornstarch

2 tbsp (30 ml) water

¼ cup (50 g) sugar

1 tsp powdered gelatin

3 tbsp (43 g) unsalted butter

Bao Dough

½ cup (120 ml) milk, cold

¾ tsp instant yeast

1½ tbsp (20 g) sugar

1⅓ cups (165 g) all-purpose flour, sifted

¼ cup (30 g) cake flour, sifted

1 tbsp (8 g) pumpkin powder, or 2 drops yellow food coloring (optional)

1½ tsp (7 ml) neutral oil or melted unsalted butter

To make the filling, first steam the salted yolks for 10 minutes or bake at 320°F (160°C) for 15 minutes. In a blender or food processor, blend the cooked salted eggs into fine crumbs, then transfer to a medium-sized bowl and combine with the custard powder, milk powder and cornstarch.

In a small saucepan, bring the water to a simmer over medium heat. Mix together the sugar and powdered gelatin, then gradually sprinkle over the water. Stir until well combined. Increase the heat to medium-high, bring the mixture to a boil, then add the butter. Stir until the butter is fully melted, then remove the mixture from the heat.

Pour the butter mixture over the salted egg mixture and stir until well combined. Cover with plastic wrap and chill the filling in the fridge for 6 hours or overnight to firm up.

Divide the filling into ten or eleven equal-sized portions, each portion being about 1 level tablespoon (15 g). Place on a plate or baking sheet, cover them with plastic wrap and keep them in the fridge until needed.

To make the bao dough, in a medium-sized bowl, combine the milk, instant yeast, sugar, all-purpose flour, cake flour, pumpkin powder (if using) and oil. Mix with a wooden spoon or spatula until no dry flour remains. Transfer the dough to a clean work surface and knead for 10 to 12 minutes, or until it becomes smooth and elastic.

Divide the dough into ten or eleven equal-sized portions, about 2 level tablespoons (30 g) each. Cover with plastic wrap or a damp, clean towel to prevent drying out.

(continued)

Salted Egg Yolk Lava Bao Buns (Continued)

Working with five doughs at a time, knead each for 2 to 3 minutes until soft and pliable with a smooth texture. Use your palms to tuck and press until a ball is formed. Place the ball smooth side down and roll it out into a 3-inch (7.5-cm)-diameter circle with thin edges and a thick center. Repeat with the remaining dough.

Place the filling in the middle of the dough, wrap the edges around the filling to cover it and make sure the seam is tightly sealed to prevent leaks while steaming. Then, use your palms to rotate and elongate the dough ball as high as possible to prevent it from flattening when steamed. Place each bun inside a paper liner that has been placed in a mini tart mold. Repeat the process with the remaining dough and filling.

Fill the steamer pot with water to a 1½-inch (4-cm) depth. Heat the water to a temperature of 110°F (45°C) and then turn off the heat. Place the buns in the steamer basket and place the basket on top of the pot. Partially cover with the lid opened by about ½ inch (1.3 cm). Let the buns proof for 30 to 45 minutes, or until they have increased in size by 60 percent. You can test whether they are ready by gently pressing the surface of a bun and observing if it slowly rises again.

Remove the steamer basket from the pot and bring the water in the pot to a boil over high heat. Then, lower the heat to medium. To prevent water droplets from falling on the buns during steaming, wrap the steamer lid with a clean cloth. Place the basket of proofed buns over the pot, cover fully and steam for 8 minutes.

Once the steaming is done, turn off the heat and let the bao buns sit in the steamer basket for 5 minutes to keep them from collapsing. Then, open the lid and take them out of the steamer to serve.

It is best to eat lava buns right after they are steamed, since the filling will still be runny and ooze out of the bun when torn. But they can also be served at room temperature, although the filling will thicken and no longer be as runny. The leftover buns can be stored in a sealed container or ziplock bag in the fridge for up to 2 days or in the freezer for about a month. To reheat the buns, simply steam them for 5 minutes.

Durian Bao Buns (Banh Bao Mui Sau Rieng)

Yield:
8 buns

Southeast Asians have a special love for durian, a fruit that is highly esteemed and valued. In Vietnam, we incorporate durian into various sweet dishes and desserts, including durian bao buns, which are one-of-a-kind treats. With this recipe, you can create bao buns that resemble golden durian pulp and are filled with a creamy and intensely fragrant durian custard. If you appreciate the unique flavor and aroma of durian, this is a combination that you don't want to miss.

Durian Custard Filling

1 large egg

⅓ cup (67 g) sugar

1 tbsp (5 g) milk powder

1 tbsp (8 g) cornstarch or cake flour

¼ cup (60 ml) milk

¼ cup (60 ml) coconut milk

2 tbsp (28 g) unsalted butter

4 oz (115 g) durian flesh, mashed finely

Bao Dough

½ cup (120 ml) milk, cold

¾ tsp instant yeast

1½ tbsp (20 g) sugar

1⅓ cups (165 g) all-purpose flour, sifted

¼ cup (30 g) cake flour, sifted

1 tbsp (8 g) pumpkin powder, or 2 drops yellow food coloring (optional)

1½ tsp (7 ml) neutral oil or melted unsalted butter

To make the durian custard filling, in a medium-sized bowl, whisk together the egg and sugar until well combined. Then, add the milk powder and cornstarch and stir to combine. In a small saucepan, combine the milk, coconut milk and butter. Stir the mixture over medium-low heat to melt the butter and bring the mixture to a simmer. Remove the mixture from the heat and slowly pour in the egg mixture while stirring constantly until everything is well mixed. Strain the mixture through a fine-mesh sieve into the previous saucepan.

Stir the mixture over medium-low heat for 8 to 10 minutes, until it thickens, becomes smooth and pliable and no longer sticks to the pan. Once thick, turn off the heat and add the mashed durian flesh, mixing until everything is well combined. Transfer the durian custard to a heatproof container, cover with plastic wrap and allow to cool completely before refrigerating for an hour.

Divide the filling into eight equal-sized portions of about 1 heaping tablespoon (19 g) each. Place on a plate or baking sheet, cover them with plastic wrap and keep in the fridge until needed.

To make the bao dough, in a medium-sized bowl, combine the milk, instant yeast, sugar, all-purpose flour, cake flour, pumpkin powder (if using) and oil. Mix well with a wooden spoon or spatula until no dry flour remains. Transfer the dough to a clean work surface and knead for 10 to 12 minutes, or until it becomes smooth and elastic.

Divide the dough into eight equal-sized portions, each consisting of about 3 tablespoons (45 g). Cover with plastic wrap or a damp, clean towel to prevent drying out. Working with one dough ball at a time, knead a dough ball for 2 to 3 minutes, or until soft and pliable with a smooth texture. Use your palms to tuck and press until a ball is formed. Place the smooth side down and roll it out into a 4-inch (10-cm)-diameter circle with thin edges and a thick center.

(continued)

Durian Bao Buns (Continued)

Place a portion of the durian filling in the center of the dough, wrap the edges to cover the filling and seal the seam tightly. Form the dough into a shape that resembles the whole durian pulp. Place each bun in a paper cupcake liner or on parchment paper, and repeat the process with the remaining dough and filling.

Fill the steamer pot with water to a 1½-inch (4-cm) depth. Heat the water to a temperature of 110°F (45°C) and then turn off the heat. Place the buns in the steamer basket and place the basket on top of the pot. Partially cover with the lid opened by about ½ inch (1.3 cm). Let the buns proof for 60 minutes, or until they have increased in size by 60 percent. You can test whether they are ready by gently pressing the surface of a bun and observing if it slowly rises again.

Remove the steamer basket from the pot and bring the water in the pot to a boil over high heat. Then, lower the heat to medium. To prevent water droplets from falling on the buns during steaming, wrap the steamer lid with a clean cloth. Place the basket of proofed buns over the pot, cover fully and steam for 8 minutes.

Once the steaming is done, turn off the heat and let the bao buns sit in the steamer basket for 5 minutes to keep them from collapsing. Then, open the lid and remove them from the steamer to serve.

For the best experience, it's recommended to consume the custard buns when they are warm. The leftover durian buns can be stored in a sealed container or ziplock bag in the fridge for up to 2 days, or in the freezer for about a month. To reheat the buns, simply steam them for 5 minutes.

Boba, Jellies and Ice Creams

Last but not least, the final chapter of my book is all about chilled desserts, which hold a special place in Vietnamese cuisine due to the year-round hot climate.

Here, you will discover how easy it is to make some of the popular pearls at home, which are commonly used in milk tea. Additionally, you will learn how to create unique Vietnamese-flavored jellies, such as coconut and coffee, which can be combined with flan for an extra layer of flavor. And, of course, no dessert list would be complete without mentioning ice cream. Banana ice cream (page 149) is a simple and nostalgic dish that many Vietnamese associate with their childhood. Recently, avocado with coconut ice cream (page 146) has become a hit, particularly in Da Lat, a foggy city located in the Central Highlands province of Vietnam. These chilled desserts are a must-try when visiting Vietnam, and with the recipes provided, you can enjoy them from the comfort of your own home.

Frozen Yogurt with Tapioca Pearls in Coconut Milk Sauce (Sua Chua Tran Chau Nuoc Cot Dua)

Frozen yogurt with tapioca pearls is an interesting and creative dish that has only appeared in Vietnam in the past few years and is well received by young people as well as sweets enthusiasts. This sweet dish includes three main ingredients: frozen yogurt, chewy tapioca pearls and a warm coconut milk sauce. The seemingly opposite combination of the temperatures and textures create a unique, delicious dish.

Yield:
6 servings

Frozen Yogurt

2 cups (475 ml) heavy cream

3 cups (690 g) plain yogurt

¾ cup (180 ml) sweetened condensed milk

Tapioca Pearls

¼ cup (60 ml) water

2 tbsp (36 g) sugar

½ cup (60 g) + 2 tbsp (16 g) tapioca starch, divided, plus more if needed

Coconut Milk Sauce (page 14), for serving

Shredded unsweetened coconut and toasted coconut flakes, for serving

To make the frozen yogurt, in a cold and clean bowl, whisk the cream until it thickens and forms firm peaks. Then, mix in the yogurt and condensed milk until the mixture is smooth and fully combined. Finally, pour the mixture into a food container and freeze for at least 8 hours or overnight, until it becomes fully frozen.

To make the tapioca pearls, in a small saucepan, mix together the water, sugar and 1 tablespoon (8 g) of tapioca starch. Stir the mixture over medium heat until it thickens to a sticky, transparent consistency, then turn off the heat. Add ½ cup (60 g) of the tapioca starch and mix until well combined. Knead with your hands until you have a smooth, nonsticky dough. If your dough is still sticky, add some tapioca starch. If it's still dry, some hot water should do the trick.

Divide the dough into four or five equal-sized pieces, then roll each piece into a long rope about ⅜ inch (1 cm) thick. Cut the ropes into small pieces and roll each piece into a pearl that is about ⅜ inch (1 cm) in diameter. Finally, evenly coat the pearls with the remaining tablespoon (8 g) of tapioca starch to keep them from sticking together.

Bring a medium-sized saucepan of water to a boil over medium heat, then add the pearls. Cook them for about 20 minutes, or until they float to the surface. Once the pearls have floated, turn off the heat, cover the pot and let them incubate for 30 minutes to thoroughly cook them. After that, transfer to a bowl of cold water to cool.

Add the pearls to the prepared coconut milk sauce and keep warm at approximately 160°F (70°C). To serve, place some scoops of the frozen yogurt in a dessert bowl and top them with warm tapioca pearls in coconut milk sauce. Sprinkle shredded coconut or toasted coconut flakes on top.

Brown Sugar Bubble Tea
(Tra Sua Tran Chau Duong Den)

Yield:
4 servings

Pearl milk tea, one of the most popular drinks in Vietnam, features chewy brown sugar pearls infused with the sweetness of brown sugar syrup perfectly paired with a cup of creamy and fragrant milk tea. Brown sugar pearls can be easily prepared and stored in the freezer, ready to be boiled and added to homemade milk tea for a convenient and cost-effective treat.

Brown Sugar Tapioca Pearls and Syrup

½ cup (120 ml) water, divided

¾ cup (165 g) dark brown sugar, divided

⅔ cup (79 g) + 2 tbsp (16 g) tapioca starch, divided, plus more if needed

2 tbsp (10 g) unsweetened cocoa powder

Milk Tea

2 oz (60 g) loose black tea

2½ cups (600 ml) boiling water

½ cup (100 g) sugar

2 cups (475 ml) milk

½ cup (60 g) powdered nondairy creamer

Ice cubes, for serving

To make brown sugar tapioca pearls, in a small saucepan, combine ¼ cup (60 ml) of the water, ½ cup (110 g) of the brown sugar and 1 tablespoon (8 g) of the tapioca starch from the ⅔ cup (79 g) you measured. Stir the mixture over medium heat until it thickens to a sticky, translucent consistency, then turn off the heat. Add the remaining tapioca starch from the ⅔ cup (79 g) and the cocoa powder, and mix until well combined. Knead with your hands until you have a smooth, nonsticky dough. If your dough is still sticky, add some tapioca starch. If it's still dry, some hot water should do the trick.

Divide the dough into four to five equal-sized pieces, then roll each piece into a long rope about ⅜ inch (1 cm) thick. Cut the ropes into small pieces and roll each piece into a pearl that is about ⅜ inch (1 cm) in diameter. Finally, evenly coat the pearls with the remaining 2 tablespoons (16 g) of tapioca starch to keep them from sticking together.

Bring a medium-sized saucepan of water to a boil over medium heat, then add the pearls. Cook them for about 20 minutes, or until they float to the surface. Once the pearls have floated, turn off the heat, cover the pot and let them incubate for 30 minutes to thoroughly cook them. After that, transfer to a bowl of cold water to cool.

To make the brown sugar syrup, in a small saucepan, combine the remaining ¼ cup (55 g) of brown sugar and ¼ cup (60 ml) of water. Heat the mixture over medium heat until it comes to a boil. Lower the heat to medium-low and let simmer for an additional 5 minutes. Turn off the heat and let the syrup cool to 140°F (60°C). Once cooled, add the drained pearls to the syrup and soak for at least 30 minutes before using.

To make the milk tea, in a medium-sized saucepan, combine the black tea and boiling water. Let the tea steep for 10 minutes, then strain the mixture through a strainer, removing the tea leaves. Next, add the sugar, milk and nondairy creamer, and stir well. Adjust the sweetness to taste.

To serve, place brown sugar pearls into a glass, add ice cubes and pour the milk tea on top. Don't forget to use a large boba straw!

Silky Tofu Pudding with Tapioca Pearls in Ginger Syrup (Tao Pho Nuoc Duong)

Tao pho (tofu) is a popular childhood delicacy in Vietnam, with various ways of savoring it depending on the region. This dish is made from pure soy milk and has an ivory white color and a smooth, light texture that melts in your mouth. In the North, it is enjoyed with rock sugar syrup and fresh jasmine flowers for a refreshing taste. In Central Vietnam, it is mixed with granulated sugar, lemon juice and crushed ginger to produce a harmonious sweet and spicy flavor. In the South, it is combined with palm sugar–ginger syrup, chewy tapioca pearls and creamy coconut milk sauce for a warm and creative dish. This recipe will guide you in making the southern style.

Yield:
6 servings

Tofu Pudding

8 oz (225 g) soybeans

5 cups (scant 1.2 L) + 3 tbsp (45 ml) water, divided

5 pandan leaves (optional)

3 tbsp (25 g) cornstarch

½ tsp glucono-delta-lactone (GDL) (see page 153)

2 tsp (10 ml) water, boiled then cooled

To make the tofu pudding, wash the soybeans, then soak them in 1 quart (946 ml) of water for 6 to 8 hours to soften them. After soaking, remove any silk skin and drain the beans thoroughly.

In a blender, blend the softened beans with 2 cups (475 ml) of fresh water to make a smooth mixture. Strain the mixture through a piece of cheesecloth into a medium-sized bowl to separate the soy milk from the bean residue. Place the residue in a separate large bowl, add 3 cups (710 ml) of the remaining water and squeeze once more through the cheesecloth, over the bowl of already strained soy milk, to extract additional soy milk.

Pour the soy milk into a medium-sized saucepan and add the pandan leaves (if using). Cook over medium-low heat for 5 to 7 minutes. While the milk is cooking, stir it constantly and remove any foam that rises to the surface. Remove and discard the pandan leaves and continue to cook the soy milk for 10 more minutes.

In a cup, mix the cornstarch with the remaining 3 tablespoons (45 ml) of water, then slowly pour it into the soy milk while stirring, until the two are well combined. Cook the mixture for another 3 to 5 minutes, then turn off the heat and remove any lumps that may have formed on the surface.

In a large clean, dry bowl, mix the GDL with the boiled and cooled water. Tilt the bowl so the mixture can coat the inside evenly. Pour the hot soy milk mixture through a sieve into the bowl to remove any milk residue. Remove any foam from the surface to ensure a smooth texture. Place a thin, clean towel over the bowl and cover with a lid. Let the tofu set for 40 minutes without moving the bowl.

(continued)

Silky Tofu Pudding with Tapioca Pearls in Ginger Syrup (Continued)

Tapioca Pearls

¼ cup (60 ml) water

2 tbsp (26 g) granulated sugar

½ cup (60 g) + 2 tbsp (16 g) tapioca starch, divided, plus more if needed

Ginger Syrup

8 oz (225 g) palm or cane sugar

1½ cups (355 ml) water

1 oz (30 g) fresh ginger, peeled and sliced

While the tofu sets, to make the tapioca pearls, in a small saucepan, combine the water, sugar and 1 tablespoon (8 g) of tapioca starch. Stir the mixture over medium heat until it thickens to a sticky, transparent consistency, then turn off the heat. Add ½ cup (60 g) of the tapioca starch and mix until well combined. Knead with your hands until you have a smooth, nonsticky dough. If your dough is still sticky, add some tapioca starch. If it's still dry, some hot water should do the trick.

Divide the dough into four or five equal-sized pieces, then roll each piece into a long rope about ⅜ inch (1 cm) thick. Cut the ropes into small pieces and roll each piece into a pearl that is about ⅜ inch (1 cm) in diameter. Finally, evenly coat the pearls with the remaining tablespoon (8 g) of tapioca starch to keep them from sticking together.

Bring a medium-sized saucepan of water to a boil over medium heat, then add the pearls. Cook them for about 20 minutes, or until they float to the surface. Once the pearls have floated, turn off the heat, cover the pot and let them incubate for 30 minutes to thoroughly cook them. After that, transfer to a bowl of cold water to cool.

To make the ginger syrup, in a small saucepan, combine the palm sugar and water. Stir the mixture over medium-low heat until the sugar is dissolved and the syrup comes to a boil. Add the sliced ginger and cook for another 5 to 7 minutes, or until the syrup is slightly sticky. Add the pearls and keep the ginger syrup mixture warm at around 160°F (70°C).

When the tofu has set, ladle it into a dessert bowl, add the ginger syrup and pearls on top, and serve while it's still hot. You can cut a soft-drink can in half diagonally and use it to scoop up the tofu like Vietnamese people do.

Layered Coffee and Flan Cheese Jelly
(Rau Cau Ca Phe Flan Pho Mai)

Yield:
6 servings

In Vietnam, if you're looking for a sweet dessert or a delicious beverage, you can't go wrong with flan or coffee. As a result, the Vietnamese have combined these two popular foods into a unique jelly that combines the exquisite flavors of both. This jelly has multiple layers that are stacked and intertwined, creating a visually stunning and mouthwatering treat.

Jelly Base

1 tbsp (9 g) agar-agar powder

4¼ cups (1 L) water

1 tbsp (9 g) konnyaku jelly powder (see page 150)

1 cup (200 g) sugar

Pinch of salt

Coffee Mixture

4 tbsp (20 g) instant coffee powder

1½ cups (355 ml) boiling water

Flan Cheese Mixture

4 oz (115 g) cream cheese, at room temperature

3 large egg yolks

⅓ cup (80 ml) sweetened condensed milk

1 tsp vanilla extract

1 cup (240 ml) milk

In a small saucepan off the heat, combine the agar-agar powder and water and stir well. If you have time, let the agar-agar powder soak in water for 1 hour. Otherwise, just let it soak for about 15 minutes. Soaking the agar-agar powder before cooking is a way to keep your finished jelly less runny after a few days in the fridge.

Meanwhile, to make the coffee mixture, in a small heatproof bowl, stir the coffee powder into the boiling water until it dissolves.

To make the flan cheese mixture, in a small bowl, cream the cream cheese until smooth, then mix in the egg yolks, condensed milk and vanilla until everything is well combined. Next, in a small saucepan, heat the milk and pour it into the cheese mixture, stirring continuously until everything is well mixed. Run the mixture through a fine-mesh sieve into the same small saucepan to make it smoother. Stir the mixture over low heat for about 3 minutes, or until it becomes slightly thicker. Remove from the heat and cover with a lid.

After soaking, place the saucepan with the jelly base over medium heat and cook, stirring constantly, until it starts to boil. In a small cup, mix the konnyaku jelly powder with the sugar and salt. Then, slowly add the mixture to the pot while stirring so that the jelly powder doesn't get lumpy. Let the mixture boil for 5 minutes, then remove it from the heat.

Divide the jelly base evenly between two saucepans. Pour the coffee into one of the saucepans and stir well. Place the other saucepan over low heat, add the flan cheese mixture and stir well. To prevent the jelly bases from setting, place the two saucepans over very low heat and maintain them at a warm temperature.

(continued)

Layered Coffee and Flan Cheese Jelly (Continued)

Pour a ¼-inch (6-mm) layer of the coffee mixture into a rectangular food container or mold (I used a baking pan that measured 11 inches [28 cm] long, 9 inches [23 cm] wide and 2 inches [5 cm] high) and let set for 3 to 4 minutes, or until the surface has a slight jiggle and tackiness. Carefully ladle a ¼-inch (6-mm) layer of the flan cheese mixture over the coffee layer, pouring from the edge to the center to avoid breaking the bottom layer. Let the jelly sit for 3 to 4 minutes to harden, then repeat the process for the next layers in the same order. (I layered the jelly six times in the rectangular baking pan that I used.) Let the jelly set and chill in the fridge for at least 2 hours.

To serve, remove the jelly from the mold and cut it into bite-sized pieces. The jelly can be kept in the fridge for up to 4 days in an airtight container.

Two-Layered Coconut Jelly (Rau Cau Trai Dua)

Yield:
4 servings

As Vietnam is a tropical nation, coconut is a beloved fruit and drink, and it's no surprise that it appears in many dishes both sweet and savory. Among these is a refreshing and unique coconut jelly dessert. This dessert features two layers of stacked jelly made from fresh coconut water and creamy coconut milk, served in a whole coconut. With each bite, you'll feel like you're at a "coconut party" in your mouth.

Coconut Bowl

2 fresh young coconuts (each about 5" [13 cm] in diameter)

Coconut Jelly

6 cups (1.4 L) coconut water (from fresh coconuts or store-bought)

5 pandan leaves (optional)

1 tsp konnyaku jelly powder (see page 150)

¾ cup (150 g) sugar

Pinch of salt

Coconut Milk Jelly

½ cup (120 ml) coconut milk

¼ tsp konnyaku jelly powder

1 tbsp (15 g) sugar

Place a coconut horizontally on a cutting board. With a sharp, heavy knife, cut a 3-inch (7.5-cm) circle around the top of the coconut. Sieve the coconut water into a saucepan to get the purest water possible, free of coconut shell and meat. After that, place the coconut upside down on a rack to dry off the inside coconut meat. Repeat with the second coconut. If you cannot get coconuts in their whole state, you can make the jelly in food containers or jars.

In a pot, combine 6 cups (1.4 L) of coconut water and the pandan leaves (if using) and bring to a boil over medium heat. After 3 minutes, remove the pandan leaves.

In a small bowl, combine the konnyaku jelly powder, sugar and salt. Then, slowly sprinkle this mixture into the pot of coconut water while stirring to keep the jelly powder from clumping. Let boil for another 5 minutes, then remove from the heat.

Divide the coconut jelly mixture evenly between the 2 coconuts, propping them upright and filling them up to about ¾ inch (2 cm) from the opening of the shell. Let the jelly sit at room temperature for 10 to 15 minutes, or until it has partially set and has a slight elasticity when touched.

Meanwhile, to make the coconut milk jelly, in a small saucepan, simmer the coconut milk over medium-low heat. In a small bowl, mix the konnyaku jelly powder and sugar together, then slowly sprinkle the mixture into the coconut milk. Stir constantly to keep the jelly powder from getting lumpy. Remove from the heat and transfer to a pouring cup.

Top the mixture in the shells with the coconut milk jelly, then refrigerate until fully firm. Serve the chilled coconut jelly to fully appreciate the refreshing taste of fresh coconut water and the rich sweetness of coconut milk.

Avocado Smoothie with Coconut Ice Cream
(Kem Bo)

With its tropical monsoon climate, Vietnam stays hot and humid throughout the year, making ice cream and chilled beverages favorites among locals. This deliciously cool, creamy coconut ice cream paired with a silky-smooth avocado smoothie is a beloved sweet treat among Vietnamese people. Despite its simplicity, this recipe is sure to surprise and delight your taste buds.

Coconut Ice Cream

½ cup (120 ml) coconut milk

½ cup (120 ml) sweetened condensed milk

¼ cup (25 g) desiccated coconut

1 tbsp (8 g) cornstarch

¼ tsp salt

1 cup (240 ml) heavy cream

Avocado Smoothie

1 lb (455 g) avocado flesh, diced

½ cup (120 ml) sweetened condensed milk

¼ cup (60 ml) milk

¼ cup (60 ml) heavy cream

Toasted coconut flakes, for serving

Shredded unsweetened coconut, for serving

Toasted peanuts, for serving

To make coconut ice cream, in a small saucepan, combine the coconut milk, condensed milk, desiccated coconut, cornstarch and salt. Stir the mixture constantly over medium-low heat for 5 to 7 minutes, or until it thickens. Remove from the heat and let cool completely.

In a large cold, clean bowl, whisk the cream until it thickens and forms firm peaks. Then, stir in the cooled coconut mixture until all the ingredients are smooth and fully combined. Finally, pour the mixture into a food container and freeze for at least 8 hours or overnight, until it becomes fully frozen.

To make the avocado smoothie, in a blender, blend the diced avocado with the condensed milk, milk and heavy cream until smooth. To serve, divide the avocado smoothie equally between three or four dessert glasses, then add two scoops of coconut ice cream to each glass. Sprinkle some toasted coconut flakes, shredded coconut and toasted peanuts over the ice cream.

Banana with Coconut Ice Cream (Kem Chuoi)

Yield:
14 servings

Banana ice cream is a nostalgic treat associated with childhood for many people of Generation Y in Vietnam. During hot summer afternoons, children would rush out to buy banana ice cream pops from vendors that contained bananas with coconut milk, roasted peanuts and grated coconut pressed in a nylon bag. It's a rustic and idyllic treat that brings back fond memories.

14 bananas

1 cup (145 g) peanuts

1 tbsp (18 g) + ⅛ tsp salt, divided

2 cups (475 ml) coconut milk

½ cup (120 ml) sweetened condensed milk

2 tbsp (15 g) tapioca starch

5 oz (140 g) shredded unsweetened coconut

To make the banana ice cream, peel the bananas and insert a wooden ice cream stick into each one. Place the bananas in small individual ziplock bags that measure approximately 3 x 4 inches (7.5 x 10 cm). Use a cutting board or large knife to press down and flatten the bananas until they are about ⅜ inch (1 cm) thick. Chill the bananas in the fridge while you prepare the other ingredients. If you prefer not to use ziplock bags, you can use ice cream molds or a food container as an alternative.

To make the peanut topping, place a small nonstick skillet over low heat and add the peanuts and 1 tablespoon (18 g) of the salt. Stir constantly and roast the peanuts until fragrant and golden. Then, remove from the heat and allow the peanuts to cool down before rubbing off and discarding their skin and crumbling them with a rolling pin.

For the cream sauce, in a small saucepan, combine the coconut milk, condensed milk, tapioca starch, remaining ⅛ teaspoon of salt and shredded coconut. Cook over low heat, stirring constantly, for 7 to 10 minutes, or until thickened. Remove from the heat and let cool completely.

To assemble, open the mouth of a banana bag and spoon in the prepared cream sauce. Sprinkle crushed peanuts on both sides, then reseal the bag. Repeat the process with the remaining bananas and freeze the ice cream for at least 8 hours or overnight.

To enjoy this tasty treat, simply remove the ziplock bags from the freezer when ready to serve.

A Guide to Vietnamese Ingredients

If you are new to Southeast Asian cuisine, you may find some of the ingredients used in these recipes quite unfamiliar. I understand that this can be confusing, so I have created this list to introduce some of the Vietnamese and Southeast Asian ingredients used in this book. My hope is that through my explanations, you will gain a better understanding of these ingredients and be able to adjust and substitute for them when preparing the recipes. You can find these ingredients at Asian grocery stores or on Amazon.

Peeled split mung beans: This is a popular type of bean in Vietnam. They are produced by removing the green silk skin from the mung beans, which reveals their yellow color. Typically, they are boiled or steamed, and when cooked, they offer a natural, light sweetness, smooth texture and nutty taste. Cooked beans can be blended with other ingredients such as milk, coconut milk and sugar to create a smooth mixture used for ice cream or pudding. By stirring the mung bean puree over medium-low heat in a nonstick pan, the steam will evaporate and cause it to thicken like a paste. This resulting paste can also be used as a cake filling or sweet soup ingredient.

Pandan leaves: Pandan leaves are long, narrow and straight, measuring 12 to 13 inches (30 to 33 cm) long with a sharp, bladelike tip. They are commonly grown in Southeast Asia and widely used as a cooking ingredient. To prepare, the white part of the leaves is removed, and the green part is cut into small pieces, blended with water and then squeezed to extract the green juice. The resulting pandan leaf juice is used to add a green color to cakes, sticky rice, jellies and other desserts. Pandan leaves have a unique and delightful aroma, often referred to as the "vanilla of Southeast Asia." They are commonly used to add fragrance to sweet soups, sauces, rice and sticky rice. Fresh or frozen pandan leaves can be purchased for similar results.

Salted egg yolks: Salted eggs are a preserved type of egg, commonly duck egg, that are soaked in brine or packed in salted charcoal to increase their shelf life. They can be purchased whole or as separated egg yolks. To prepare whole salted eggs, you need to wash off the black charcoal outer shell, break the eggs and remove the yolks, which should be rinsed gently under clean running water. To reduce the smell of the eggs, you can soak them in rice wine for about 5 minutes before rinsing with clean water. Salted egg yolks can be steamed for 7 minutes or baked at 320°F (160°C) for 7 minutes, and you can add a thin layer of sesame oil to make them smell good. Baking produces more visually appealing salted egg yolks and is often done when using salted eggs to decorate cakes or as a filling for mooncakes. The steaming method is more suitable if you want to use salted egg yolks as a sauce or as a filling for bao buns or breads.

Konnyaku jelly powder: This is a popular jelly-making powder in Vietnam, in addition to agar-agar powder. In contrast to agar-agar powder, which is made from red seaweed and produces a firm and hard jelly texture, konnyaku jelly powder is made from the root vegetable konjac, resulting in a chewy, supple and jiggly texture. Konnyaku jelly powder can be used as a vegan-friendly substitute for gelatin, making it a versatile option for creating delicious desserts.

Golden syrup: Golden syrup, also known as light treacle, is a thick amber-colored syrup that resembles honey. It is created by inverting sugar during the refining process, using only cane sugar, water and citric acid. In Vietnam, golden syrup is an indispensable ingredient used to create the crust of baked mooncakes. It gives the mooncakes a beautiful golden brown color, enhancing their aroma, softness and deep flavor. Additionally, golden syrup can also be used as a liquid sweetener to make various cakes and desserts.

Meat floss: Meat floss is a type of dried meat product made from lean pork or chicken breast. It has a light and fluffy texture and is typically named after the meat it is made from, such as pork floss or chicken floss. To make meat floss at home, the meat is first cooked with spices, torn into small pieces and then pounded with a pestle. The mixture is then dried on a pan over low heat until it becomes completely dry. Meat floss typically has a salty and mildly sweet taste and may even be spicy. The color of the floss can vary from light yellow to red-orange depending on the spices used in the cooking process. It is commonly used as a topping for breads and salted egg sponge cakes, or served with rice or white porridge.

Sago: Mini tapioca pearls, also known as sago, are a powder made from cassava that takes the form of small round milky-white granules. Once cooked, sago turns transparent, slightly soft and chewy. Sago is often used to create a desirable consistency and stickiness in sweet soups, desserts and cakes, providing a pleasant texture and mouthfeel when chewed.

Cassava sticks: Cassava sticks are a dried product made from cassava powder. They typically come in long serrated bars and have a translucent appearance. When cooked, they become transparent and have a soft, chewy texture similar to sago. In Vietnam, cassava sticks are often used to create a delightful, chewy texture in sweet soups.

Coix seeds: Coix seeds, also known as adlay, pearl barley or Job's tears, have a small, slightly rounded grain shape and are typically ivory-white in color. Vietnamese cuisine uses coix seeds in many sweet soups and desserts, such as the Refreshing Herbal Dessert Drink (Che Sam Bo Luong, page 63), which is believed to help purify and cool the body. Although coix seeds offer many health benefits, they are inherently very hard and require soaking for an extended period of time or stewing on the stove for a long time to soften the seeds before they can be used in cooking.

Dried lotus seeds: Dried lotus seeds are the seeds of the lotus plant that have been processed and dried. They have a milky-white color and, when cooked, give off a pleasant aroma. They have a fleshy texture and easily melt in the mouth when eaten. Dried lotus seeds are highly nutritious and offer many health benefits. Vietnamese cuisine often incorporates lotus seeds in dishes and desserts as they are believed to help clear heat and detoxify the body.

Dried longans: Dried longan is produced by drying longan pulp after preliminary processing. The resulting fruit is typically golden brown or amber in color, with a wrinkled and rough outer skin and shiny inner flesh. When consumed, dried longans offer a unique combination of softness, flexibility, sweetness and a distinctive light aroma. In addition to its pleasant taste and texture, dried longan is known for its health benefits. It is often used in combination with other ingredients to make healthy sweet soups and desserts.

Dried jujubes: Dried jujubes are harvested jujubes that have been dried. They are dark red, slightly wrinkled on the outside and sweet and fleshy on the inside. Dried jujubes offer numerous health benefits, including improving digestion, enhancing sleep quality, restoring physical strength and beautifying the skin. In addition to their nutritional benefits, dried jujubes are commonly used in various dishes and desserts, as well as in the preparation of herbal teas.

Dried goji berries: Dried goji berries are a popular health supplement known for enhancing liver and kidney function, brightening the eyes and improving skin. These berries are small and red or orange-red, with a wrinkled outer skin and numerous small yellow seeds inside. Dried goji berries are commonly used to make herbal teas, healthy desserts and sweet soups due to their numerous health benefits.

Dried shredded kelp: Dried shredded kelp is a type of seaweed that has been dried, resulting in a shift from dark green to gray. When soaked in water, the kelps gradually expand, soften and turn dark green. These seaweeds are known for their sweet, cool and chewy characteristics. They offer many health benefits and are commonly used in savory and sweet soups to nourish and purify the body.

Dried wood-ear mushrooms: The wood-ear mushroom, also known as tree ear due to its earlike shape, grows on decaying tree trunks and is dark brown when fresh and black when dried. Once dried, the mushrooms are hard and crispy, but after soaking, they become soft and elastic with a rubbery texture. When cooked, the mushrooms have a texture similar to shredded kelp, which makes them a good substitute for adding a chewy and crunchy texture to sweet soups. Despite their different nutritional values, wood-ear mushrooms and shredded kelp can be used interchangeably for texture purposes.

Lotus root: Lotus, a perennial herbaceous aquatic plant, has a large tubular root with many long hollow holes inside. To prepare the root for cooking, the dark outer skin is peeled off and then the root is sliced or cut into short pieces, depending on the desired dish. The root has a crunchy texture when fresh and a soft texture when cooked, with a natural, delicious sweetness. Lotus root is commonly used in Asian cuisine, where it is incorporated into a wide variety of dishes, including snacks, salads, soups, stews and desserts.

Cassava: Cassava is a root vegetable that grows widely in tropical climates. It has a rough outer skin that can be easily peeled off by hand, revealing a starchy white flesh inside. This starchy flesh is the main ingredient in tapioca starch, a powder that is commonly used to thicken soups, sauces and baked goods such as cakes. Before eating, cassava must be peeled and cooked thoroughly because raw cassava contains a relatively high concentration of cyanogenic glycosides. These can release harmful cyanide when consumed. Cassava can be used in a variety of ways, much like potatoes. It can be used to make bread, mashed potatoes, cakes or snacks. In Vietnam, cassava roots are often used to make sweet soup or traditional cakes.

Glucono-delta-lactone (GDL): Glucono-delta-lactone (GDL) is a natural food additive. It is an odorless white powder that is easily soluble in water and has a slightly sweet taste that gradually becomes sour. GDL is often used in the production of tofu in Vietnam, where it serves as a coagulant to solidify soy milk and form curds. GDL is a safe and widely accepted food additive used to regulate acidity and extend shelf life, among other purposes.

Alum powder: Alum powder, also known as potassium alum, is a white or translucent crystalline powder that is commonly used as a food additive and purifying agent. In Vietnamese cuisine, alum powder is often mixed with water and used when soaking vegetables to create a crunchy texture and prevent color darkening due to oxidation. Its uses in Vietnamese cuisine include creating a crunchy texture for candied coconut, lotus seeds, ginger and other items known as "mut Tet," making pickles and reducing the bitter taste of pomelo pith when cooking pomelo sweet soup.

Acknowledgments

First, I want to thank all of my followers of TARA's Recipes for their incredible support and encouragement. Without their backing, I would not be where I am today.

I would also like to extend my sincere thanks to Page Street Publishing for giving me the opportunity to share my passion for my country's culinary culture with readers around the world. Thank you for seeing my potential and for helping me turn my dream into reality. I want to express my deep gratitude to Franny Donington, my editor, for her unwavering support and guidance throughout this journey. Initially, I was hesitant to accept the offer to write an English manual due to not being a native English speaker. However, Franny's constant encouragement, explanations and understanding helped me overcome my doubts and insecurities. She provided invaluable feedback, always pushing me to reach my full potential and recognizing my accomplishments. I am incredibly grateful to have had her by my side, and I could not have completed this book without her. Thank you, Franny, from the bottom of my heart.

I am extremely thankful to my copyeditor, Iris Bass, whose professionalism enabled me to gain a lot of knowledge throughout the book's completion process. This book may not have been as well structured, comprehensible and user-friendly without her valuable contributions. I am also grateful to the design, marketing, production, sales, legal, accounting and technology teams at Page Street Publishing for their invaluable support and contributions to this project.

I would like to express my heartfelt gratitude to my dear friends, Ngoc and Son, for always being there to taste the many versions of cakes and recipes that I experimented with until I finally arrived at the perfect ones for this book. Their support and feedback have been invaluable to me. I also extend my thanks to Mrs. Sen, a former colleague whom I hold in high regard, for her consistent appreciation and love for my baked creations. Thank you all for being a part of this journey with me!

Thank you to my family, including my mother, father, sisters and brother, for their unwavering support and encouragement throughout the writing process of this book. Their love and care have been a constant source of motivation for me, and I am forever grateful to have them in my life. I love you all so much!

Thank you, Thuat, my soulmate, for being my pillar of support throughout this journey. You have always been by my side, providing me with comfort, encouragement and care, especially during the times when I was too absorbed in writing this book to take care of myself. You have tried every single cake that I made, even though you don't have a sweet tooth, and your feedback has been invaluable to me. Thank you for always treating me like a princess and for being my rock. I appreciate and love you more than words can express.

Finally, I would like to thank myself for taking the leap of faith and embarking on this incredible journey. Thank you for believing in yourself and having the courage to pursue your dream of writing a book. Thank you for persevering through the challenging moments and dedicating countless hours to this project. Thank you for continuously learning and striving to improve your skills. Most important, thank you for not giving up, even when it felt like an impossible task. You should be proud of yourself and all that you have accomplished. Thank you, myself, for all that you have done to make this book a reality.

About the Author

Tara Nguyen is a talented baking and culinary enthusiast based in Vietnam. Her passion for baking started as a hobby and quickly developed into a full-fledged career. With over five years of experience in the baking industry, Tara has had the opportunity to refine her craft and gain extensive knowledge and expertise in the field. She is known for her passion for baking and her dedication to sharing her knowledge with others.

As a food blogger and researcher, TARA's Recipes has become a popular resource for baking enthusiasts. Through her platforms on YouTube, Facebook, Instagram and TikTok, she has been able to connect with a large following who appreciate her approachable style, creative cakes and desserts and mix of cuisines. Her baking videos are of the highest quality, meticulously crafted to provide the best possible image and sound. Her blog page has become a reference for anyone who wants to explore the world of desserts and cakes, particularly in Vietnam.

In addition to her blog, Tara loves to share her recipes and knowledge of baking with her audiences in major food-loving communities in Vietnam, earning the attention and love of a large number of people.

With her book, Tara continues to share her passion for baking with more readers, introducing Vietnam's rich cultural heritage and unique flavors. Her recipes are a blend of traditional techniques and modern variations, making them accessible to both novice and experienced bakers alike. Join Tara on this culinary journey and discover the wonders of Vietnamese cuisine.

Index